# Trends and Patterns

## Helen Eccles

Series editor
**Fred Webber**

CAMBRIDGE
UNIVERSITY PRESS

PUBLISHED BY THE PRESS SYNDICATE OF THE UNIVERSITY OF CAMBRIDGE
The Pitt Building, Trumpington Street, Cambridge CB2 1RP, United Kingdom

CAMBRIDGE UNIVERSITY PRESS
The Edinburgh Building, Cambridge CB2 2RU, United Kingdom
40 West 20th Street, New York, NY 10011-4211, USA
10 Stamford Road, Oakleigh, Melbourne 3166, Australia

First published 1996
Reprinted 1996, 1997

Printed in the United Kingdom at the University Press, Cambridge

*A catalogue record for this book is available from the British Library*

ISBN 0 521 42206 X paperback

Designed and produced by Gecko Ltd, Bicester, Oxon

This book is one of a series produced to support individual
modules within the Cambridge Modular Sciences scheme.
Teachers should note that written examinations will be set
on the content of each module as defined in the syllabus.
This book is the author's interpretation of the module.

Front cover photograph: Light micrograph of nickel(II) oxide globules;
Michael W Davidson/Science Photo Library

# Contents

# Acknowledgements

8, The Natural History Museum, London; 9, courtesy of Rolls-Royce plc, Photographic and Video Services, Derby; 10*tl*, *cl*, *bl*, Dr Jeremy Burgess/Science Photo Library; 10*r*, Adam Hart-Davis/Science Photo Library; 11*t*, courtesy of Lola Cars Limited/photo: © Sutton Photographic; 11*b*, 12, Michael Brooke; 13, Science Photo Library; 32, 56, Steve Davey/La Belle Aurore; 33, 41, Ann Ronan at Image Select; 42*t*, Leslie Garland Picture Library; 42*b*, Peter Gould; 48, Sutton Photographic; 50, courtesy of Intel Corporation (UK) Ltd

# Chapter one

# Different types of matter

### By the end of this chapter you should be able to:

1 use the kinetic theory of matter to describe the changes in state between solids, liquids and gases;

2 define an ideal gas and a real gas, and understand the differences between them;

3 state the gas laws and the ideal gas equation;

4 use the ideal gas equation and the gas laws in calculations involving gases under different conditions, and in the calculation of the relative molecular mass of a gas;

5 explain the properties of silicon(IV) oxide in terms of its giant molecular structure;

6 describe and interpret the uses of aluminium, copper and some of their alloys in terms of their physical properties;

7 appreciate that materials are a finite resource and understand the importance of recycling.

In this chapter we will study three types of substances with widely different structures – gases (made up of individual molecules), silicon(IV) oxide (which has a giant covalent structure) and metals (which have a giant metallic structure). In each case we will see how the different structure of each substance gives it its own unique properties.

## The kinetic theory of matter

The kinetic theory of matter states that all matter is made up of **particles,** and exists in solid, liquid and gaseous states *(figure 1.1)*.

In the solid state the particles are packed together in an ordered, regular arrangement, with strong bonds between the particles. When heat is applied to a solid, the heat energy eventually breaks the strong bonds between the particles and the solid melts. The regular arrangement of particles is destroyed. The liquid state therefore consists of particles that are constantly in motion, free to move past each other (although some ordered groups of particles may still remain). Some forces of attraction still exist between particles in the liquid state, but these forces are much weaker than in the solid state.

What happens when we heat a solid until it melts and becomes a liquid? When heat is applied to the solid, its temperature rises. But when the solid starts to melt, the heat supplied is now used to break apart the forces holding the particles together in the solid state. The temperature no longer rises, but stays constant until all the solid has melted, and only liquid is present *(figure 1.2)*.

If the liquid is then heated, its temperature rises. But when the liquid boils, the heat supplied breaks the forces between the liquid particles so that they become widely separated. The temperature no longer rises, but stays constant until all the liquid has become vapour *(figure 1.2)*. This is called **vaporisation,** and the substance is now in a gaseous state. The particles are free to move randomly in any direction, and forces between particles are extremely weak or non-existent.

Once all the liquid has vaporised, the temperature can rise again because the heat supplied is no longer used to break bonds. We say that there is

| SOLID | LIQUID | GAS |
|---|---|---|
| 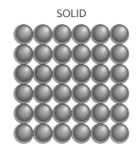 | 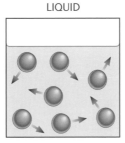 | 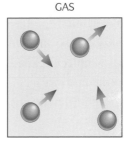 |
| particles packed together tightly – cannot move independently of each other | particles able to move past each other | particles free to move randomly |

● *Figure 1.1* The states of matter.

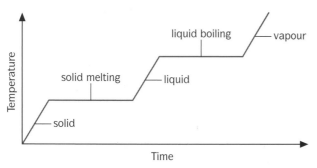

As a solid is heated, its temperature rises. While it is melting, the temperature remains steady. When all the solid has become liquid, the temperature rises again. A similar thing happens when the liquid boils.

● *Figure 1.2* The changes in temperature and phase as a solid is heated.

*no change in temperature while a material changes phase.* We see the same steady temperature for the reverse processes, at the liquefying and freezing stages. In these cases no heat is released during a phase change because bonds are being made.

In this chapter, we will look at the gaseous state and investigate how the pressure, volume and temperature of gases are inter-related.

# The kinetic theory of gases

Imagine a gas, composed of identical particles, in a closed container. How does it behave? The gas particles are in constant random motion, travelling in straight lines. They have the freedom to move and fill the fixed volume they occupy. They collide randomly with each other and with the walls of the container. This constant bombardment of the walls is the property of the gas we call **pressure**.

The collisions between the gas particles are **elastic**, which means that no energy is given out to the surroundings during a collision. A transfer of energy can occur – if a fast molecule collides with a slow molecule, the slow molecule can speed up and the fast molecule can slow down. But the total amount of kinetic energy of the molecules does not change.

## *Ideal gases*

In order to do calculations with gases, we generally assume two properties of gas particles, otherwise

the calculations can become complicated. These properties are:

■ The gas particles have mass, but zero volume – they have no size.
■ There are no internal forces between the gas particles.

Gases that behave as if they have these properties are called **ideal gases**.

All these ideas about gas particles and the way they behave constitute **the kinetic theory of gases** (*figure 1.3*).

The particles of a gas can be either atoms or molecules, but only the noble gases are composed of atoms, and in all other gases the particles are molecules. From now on, therefore, we shall assume that gas particles are molecules.

## *Real gases*

Real gases mostly behave in a very similar way to ideal gases. One difference between real gases and ideal gases can arise because of the assumption that

**Gases consist of molecules in a constant state of random motion**

■ The pressure of the gas is caused by the collisions of the molecules with the walls of the container

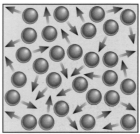 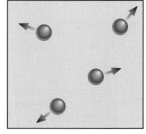

high pressure means lots of molecules, so the walls are hit many times

low pressure means few molecules, so the walls are hit only occasionally

■ The molecules travel in straight lines between collisions

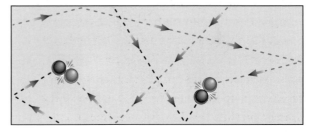

■ The total energy of the molecules does not change as a result of collisions

● *Figure 1.3* The kinetic theory of gases.

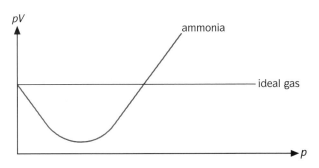

● **Figure 1.4** A graph of *pV* against *V* for both an ideal gas and ammonia. The strong intermolecular forces in ammonia mean that it does not behave like an ideal gas.

gas particles have zero volume. In a real gas the molecules *do* have a volume, but the volume of the molecules is usually so small compared with the volume of the container that it is negligible.

Another difference between real gases and ideal gases can arise because in ideal gases we assume that there are no intermolecular forces. In many real gases this is true; the intermolecular forces are negligible because the gas molecules are spread out so widely. But in gases such as ammonia, the intermolecular forces are strong, and then ideal gas behaviour is *not* shown. The graph in *figure 1.4* shows the straight line obtained for an ideal gas under different conditions of pressure (*p*) and volume (*V*). Ammonia has a very different curve, because in ammonia the bonds between the molecules are too strong to be ignored.

Under most circumstances, therefore, a real gas behaves almost exactly like an ideal gas. However, there are two extreme situations where the ideal gas model does not apply to a real gas – very high pressures and very low temperatures.

■ *High pressure*
Consider a gas at very high pressure. If the pressure is high, this means that many molecules are squeezed into the container so that the walls are constantly being bombarded with molecules and the collision rate is high. Under these circumstances the gas molecules take up a much larger proportion of the available space, so the assumption that they have no size does not apply.

The gas molecules are also very close to each other, so any attraction or repulsion between the molecules becomes more evident. We can no

longer make the assumption that internal forces do not exist.

■ *Low temperature*
Now consider a gas at a very low temperature. *Figure 1.5a* shows the behaviour of an ideal gas at constant temperature when the pressure (*p*) and volume (*V*) are changed. At any one temperature, the graph has the same shape. Each curve is called an **isotherm**.

Real gases have the same shape of isotherm as ideal gases when the temperature is high, but not at low temperatures – in this case the isotherm has a horizontal portion (*figure 1.5b*). This shows where the real gas is beginning to liquefy. This behaviour is not covered by the ideal gas equation.

Refer to the *Foundation Chemistry* module to answer these questions:

**SAQ 1.1** _____
What types of attractions exist between ammonia molecules in the gas phase?

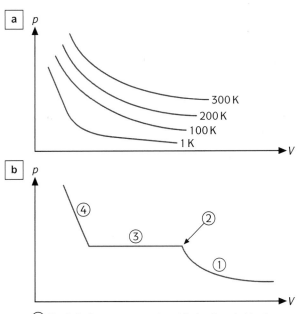

① Gas is being compressed and behaviour is ideal

② Gas is beginning to liquefy

③ Gas is changing to a liquid – the volume decreases and the pressure does not change

④ Liquid is being compressed

● **Figure 1.5 a** Isotherms for an ideal gas. **b** An isotherm at low temperature for a real gas.

## SAQ 1.2 _____

What are the particles in the gases:

a   helium;

b   oxygen;

c   nitrogen?

# The gas laws

There are three gas laws, which set out the inter-dependence of the pressure (*p*), temperature (*T*) and volume (*V*) of a gas.

## *Boyle's law*

For a fixed amount (constant number of moles) of gas, the pressure is inversely proportional to the volume if the temperature remains constant *(figure 1.6a)*:

$$p \propto \frac{1}{V} \qquad \text{at constant } T$$

## *Charles' law*

For a fixed amount of gas, the volume is proportional to the absolute temperature if the pressure remains constant *(figure 1.6b)*:

$$V \propto T \qquad \text{at constant } p$$

## *The pressure law*

For a fixed amount of gas, the pressure is proportional to the absolute temperature if the volume remains constant *(figure 1.6c)*:

$$p \propto T \qquad \text{for constant } V$$

## SAQ 1.3 _____

Use the kinetic theory of gases to explain in general terms what happens to:

a   the average speed of gas molecules when the temperature is increased;

b   the pressure of an ideal gas in a closed container when the temperature is increased;

c   the pressure of an ideal gas if the temperature is kept constant but the volume is increased.

## SAQ 1.4 _____

A Boyle's law experiment was performed with both helium and ethanoic acid vapour. The results are shown in *figure 1.7*. Helium, He, shows the closest behaviour to an ideal gas. Ethanoic acid vapour gives a curve very different to the ideal gas line. Explain.

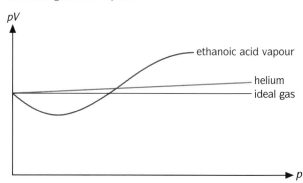

● **Figure 1.7**  Graphs of *pV* against *V* for two real gases, compared with that for an ideal gas.

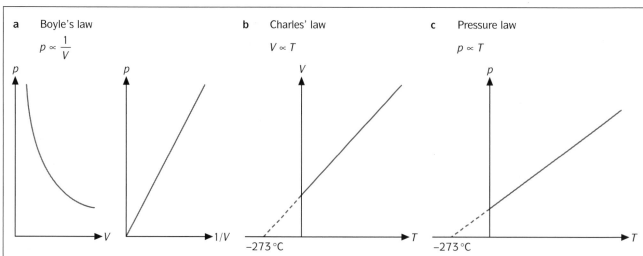

● **Figure 1.6**  The gas laws.

## Units of temperature

The temperature, $T$, in Charles' law is measured in K, the kelvin scale of temperature, and not in °C. The reason for this can be seen by looking at *figure 1.6b* – a graph of volume against temperature of an ideal gas can be extrapolated backwards to meet the temperature axis at $-273$°C. This is $0$ K, the zero of the kelvin scale of temperature. At this temperature the volume of the gas appears to be zero, which is of course impossible for real gases. The kelvin scale is used because it has no negative temperature values for a gas, and this simplifies the relationship between volume and temperature.

## Units of pressure

In the SI system of units, $1 \, \mathrm{N\,m^{-2}} \equiv 1 \, \mathrm{Pa}$ (pascal), so either of these can be used. The old unit for pressure, which is still quite often seen, is the atmosphere (atm): $1 \, \mathrm{atm} = 101.3 \, \mathrm{kPa}$ or $1.013 \times 10^5 \, \mathrm{Pa}$. Another unit of pressure is the bar, most often used in weather forecasts: $1 \, \mathrm{bar} = 100 \, \mathrm{kPa}$. Gas pressure can also be measured in terms of the height of a column of mercury supported by the gas, so the unit is millimetres of mercury (mmHg): $1 \, \mathrm{atm} = 760 \, \mathrm{mmHg}$.

## Units of volume

The SI unit of volume is the $\mathrm{m^3}$. However, we often use the $\mathrm{dm^3}$ for smaller volumes, and the $\mathrm{cm^3}$ for even smaller volumes:
$1 \, \mathrm{m^3} \equiv 1 \times 10^3 \, \mathrm{dm^3}$ and $1 \, \mathrm{dm^3} \equiv 1 \times 10^{-3} \, \mathrm{m^3}$;
$1 \, \mathrm{m^3} \equiv 1 \times 10^6 \, \mathrm{cm^3}$ and $1 \, \mathrm{cm^3} \equiv 1 \times 10^{-6} \, \mathrm{m^3}$.

# The ideal gas equation

The three gas laws,

$$pV = \text{constant} \quad \text{(at constant } T\text{)}$$
$$V/T = \text{constant} \quad \text{(at constant } p\text{)}$$
$$p/T = \text{constant} \quad \text{(at constant } V\text{)}$$

can be combined to give

$$\frac{pV}{T} = \text{constant}$$

This constant depends on the amount of gas, measured in moles. Experiments show that, if the amount of gas is doubled at constant pressure and temperature, the volume of the gas is also doubled. Therefore the constant may be written as $nR$, where $n$ is the number of moles of the gas. $R$ is the molar gas constant, which has the approximate value of $8.31 \, \mathrm{J\,K^{-1}\,mol^{-1}}$.

So we can now write an equation that shows how the pressure, volume and temperature of a gas change if the conditions are altered. This is known as the **ideal gas equation**:

$$pV = nRT$$

In this equation, $p$ = pressure of the gas (units Pa or $\mathrm{N\,m^{-2}}$), $V$ = volume of the gas (units $\mathrm{m^3}$), $n$ = number of moles of the gas, $R$ = the molar gas constant ($R$ has a value of $8.31 \, \mathrm{J\,K^{-1}\,mol^{-1}}$) and $T$ = temperature of the gas (units K).

When the ideal gas equation is used, all the quantities must be in the correct units, the units shown above. If a property of the gas is not given in these units – for instance, temperature is often given in °C and not K – it *must* be converted.

Let us look at an example. A cylinder of volume $0.5 \, \mathrm{dm^3}$ contains oxygen at $7.0 \times 10^3 \, \mathrm{kPa}$ pressure and $20$°C. How many moles of gas does the cylinder contain?

Using the ideal gas equation

$$pV = nRT$$

we have the following values:

$$p = 7.0 \times 10^3 \, \mathrm{kPa} = 7.0 \times 10^6 \, \mathrm{N\,m^{-2}}$$
$$V = 0.5 \, \mathrm{dm^3} = 0.5 \times 10^{-3} \, \mathrm{m^3}$$
$$R = 8.31 \, \mathrm{J\,K^{-1}\,mol^{-1}}$$
$$T = 20°\mathrm{C} = (273 + 20) \, \mathrm{K} = 293 \, \mathrm{K}$$

Substituting,

$$7.0 \times 10^6 \times 0.5 \times 10^{-3} = n \times 8.31 \times 293$$

$$n = \frac{7.0 \times 10^6 \times 0.5 \times 10^{-3}}{8.31 \times 293}$$

$$n = 1.4 \, \mathrm{mol}$$

If the pressure, volume and temperature of a gas change to new values because the gas has been processed, so that initial pressure $p_1 \rightarrow$ final pressure $p_2$, and similarly $V_1 \rightarrow V_2$ and $T_1 \rightarrow T_2$, then

$$\frac{p_1 V_1}{T_1} = \frac{p_2 V_2}{T_2}$$

Consider the following example. In an industrial process, nitrogen enters a container of $3 \, \mathrm{m^3}$ volume at a pressure of $101 \times 10^5$ Pa and a temperature of 300 K. It is then heated to 500 K. What is the pressure in the container at the end of the heating period?

Using

$$\frac{p_1 V_1}{T_1} = \frac{p_2 V_2}{T_2}$$

the volume remains the same, so

$$\frac{p_1}{T_1} = \frac{p_2}{T_2}$$

We have the values:

$p_1 = 101 \times 10^5$ Pa $\qquad p_2 = ?$
$T_1 = 300$ K $\qquad\qquad T_2 = 500$ K

Substituting,

$$\frac{101 \times 10^5}{300} = \frac{p_2}{500}$$

$$p_2 = \frac{101 \times 10^5 \times 500}{300}$$

$$p_2 = 168 \times 10^5 \text{ Pa}$$

## SAQ 1.5

The gas described in the example above is subsequently cooled to 100 K at the same pressure. What is the final volume of nitrogen?

## Room temperature and pressure

In gas calculations, we often consider gases at a temperature of 293 K (20°C) and a pressure of 101.3 kPa (1 atm). This combination is known as **room temperature and pressure** (r.t.p.).

Using the ideal gas equation, the volume that one mole of an ideal gas occupies at r.t.p. can be calculated. Using

$$pV = nRT$$

$$V = \frac{nRT}{p}$$

We have the values:

$n = 1$ mol
$R = 8.31 \text{ J K}^{-1} \text{mol}^{-1}$
$T = 293$ K
$p = 101.3 \text{ kPa} = 1.013 \times 10^5 \text{ Pa}$

Substituting,

$$V = \frac{1 \times 8.31 \times 293}{1.013 \times 10^5} \text{ m}^3$$

$$= 0.0240 \text{ m}^3$$
$$= 24.0 \text{ dm}^3$$

This gives us the volume that one mole of an ideal gas occupies at r.t.p.:
**1 mole of an ideal gas occupies 24.0 dm³ at r.t.p.**

Note that this applies to all ideal gases: one mole of any ideal gas occupies the same volume, 24.0 dm³, at r.t.p. It is worth remembering this important volume, because it applies to almost all gases under everyday conditions.

## Standard temperature and pressure

Sometimes, in gas calculations, you will see the term s.t.p., which means **standard temperature and pressure**. This refers to a temperature of 273 K (0°C) and a pressure of 101.3 kPa (1 atm). We use this combination of $T$ and $p$ to compare gases under the same conditions. However, you will probably use r.t.p. far more often.

Using the ideal gas equation, we can calculate the volume that 1 mole of an ideal gas occupies at standard temperature and pressure. This volume is 22.4 dm³, and again, it applies to all ideal gases:
**1 mole of an ideal gas occupies 22.4 dm³ at s.t.p.**

# Using the ideal gas equation

There are three useful ways of using the ideal gas equation.

## Using pV = nRT

What is the pressure of 2 moles of an ideal gas occupying a volume of 0.045 m³ at a temperature of 25°C?

We have:

$p = ?$
$V = 0.045 \text{ m}^3$
$n = 2$
$R = 8.31 \text{ J K}^{-1} \text{mol}^{-1}$
$T = (273 + 25) = 298$ K

Using

$$pV = nRT$$

$$p = \frac{nRT}{V}$$

Substituting,

$$p = \frac{2 \times 8.31 \times 298}{0.045}$$

$$p = 1.10 \times 10^5 \, \text{Pa}$$

## Using $p_1V_1/T_1 = p_2V_2/T_2$

A gas occupied a volume of $1 \, \text{m}^3$ at s.t.p. What volume would it occupy at $100 \times 10^5 \, \text{Pa}$ and $200 \, ^\circ\text{C}$?

We have the values

$p_1 = 1.013 \times 10^5 \, \text{Pa}$   $p_2 = 100 \times 10^5 \, \text{Pa}$
$V_1 = 1.0 \, \text{m}^3$          $V_2 = ?$
$T_1 = 273 \, \text{K}$          $T_2 = (273 + 200) = 473 \, \text{K}$

Using

$$\frac{p_1V_1}{T_1} = \frac{p_2V_2}{T_2}$$

$$V_2 = \frac{p_1V_1T_2}{T_1p_2}$$

Substituting,

$$V_2 = \frac{1.013 \times 10^5 \times 1.0 \times 473}{100 \times 10^5 \times 273}$$

$$V_2 = 0.018 \, \text{m}^3$$

## Finding the relative molecular mass ($M_r$) of a gas

In this case, the number of moles of gas is calculated using $pV = nRT$. Then, using the equation:

$$M_r = \frac{\text{mass in grams}}{\text{number of moles}} \, \text{g mol}^{-1}$$

the relative molecular mass of the gas can be calculated.

A volatile liquid with a mass of $1 \, \text{g}$ was introduced into a container of volume $2 \, \text{dm}^3$. The container was then heated until all the liquid vaporised, at $91 \, ^\circ\text{C}$. The pressure in the container was then $25.3 \, \text{kPa}$. Calculate the relative molecular mass of the liquid.

Using

$$pV = nRT$$

$$n = \frac{pV}{RT}$$

We have the values

$p = 25.3 \, \text{kPa} = 25.3 \times 10^3 \, \text{Pa}$
$V = 2.00 \, \text{dm}^3 = 2.00 \times 10^{-3} \, \text{m}^3$
$n = ?$
$R = 8.31 \, \text{J K}^{-1} \text{mol}^{-1}$
$T = (273 + 91) = 364 \, \text{K}$

Substituting,

$$n = \frac{25.3 \times 10^3 \times 2.00 \times 10^{-3}}{8.31 \times 364}$$

$$n = 0.017 \, \text{mol}$$

So the amount of gas = $0.017 \, \text{mol}$

Then, using

$$M_r = \frac{\text{mass of gas}}{\text{number of moles of gas}} \, \text{g mol}^{-1}$$

$$M_r = \frac{1.00}{0.017} = 58.8 \, \text{g mol}^{-1}$$

Therefore the relative molecular mass of the liquid is $58.8 \, \text{g mol}^{-1}$.

### SAQ 1.6
A petrol engine has a total cylinder volume of $1.50 \, \text{dm}^3$. At the top of the stroke the pressure is found to be increased by a factor of 9.0. What is the cylinder volume at the top of the stroke? (Assume the temperature is constant.)

### SAQ 1.7
An electric light bulb contains argon gas at a pressure of $0.4 \times 10^5 \, \text{Pa}$ when the temperature is $25 \, ^\circ\text{C}$. When the bulb is switched on the pressure of the argon increases to $0.7 \times 10^5 \, \text{Pa}$. What is the temperature of the gas in the light bulb when it is switched on?

### SAQ 1.8
A sample of a volatile alkane of mass $0.14 \, \text{g}$ produces $61.4 \, \text{cm}^3$ of vapour at $100 \, ^\circ\text{C}$ and standard pressure. What is the relative molecular mass of this alkane?

# Silicon(IV) oxide

Silicon(IV) oxide, $SiO_2$, is commonly called silica. It is polymorphic, which means that it exists in different crystal forms, one of which is quartz *(figure 1.8)*. Quartz is used to control the frequency of oscillators, such as those in clocks and watches. Sand is an impure form of quartz – it contains iron, which gives it a light brown colour.

The basic structure of silicon(IV) oxide is the $SiO_4$ tetrahedron *(figure 1.9)*. These tetrahedra are linked together so that they form a **giant structure**. They are linked because each O atom is part of two adjacent $SiO_4$ tetrahedra. This means that each Si atom has a half-share in its four surrounding O atoms, and each corner of the tetrahedron is shared with another tetrahedron. The average formula is therefore $SiO_2$. The bonds between the Si atoms and the shared O atoms are covalent, so the entire structure is a giant arrangement of covalently linked atoms.

Quartz has a very high melting point of 1610 °C, and does not conduct electricity or heat. These physical properties result from the extended network of covalently linked $SiO_4$ tetrahedra. The melting point is high because the covalent bonds between Si and O are strong and must be broken during the melting process. The structure does not conduct electricity because there are no delocalised electrons – the electrons form the covalent bonds and so are not free to move. Heat cannot be conducted because the atoms are held firmly by the rigid covalent bond framework – the atoms are not free to jostle their neighbours and pass on heat energy.

● *Figure 1.8* Quartz is a form of silicon(IV) oxide.

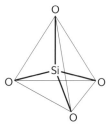

● *Figure 1.9* The $SiO_4$ tetrahedron.

**Silicates** form a complex and varied group of minerals commonly found in the Earth's crust, containing anions derived from silica, $SiO_2$. One such anion is the orthosilicate anion, $SiO_4^{4-}$, in which none of the O atoms are shared with other anions. The sharing of O atoms in silicates can be anywhere between two extremes – all four O atoms shared in silica, and no O atoms shared in the orthosilicate anion. This allows silicates a huge variety of structures such as ring, chain and sheet structures *(figure 1.10)*.

 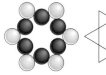

three-membered ring $(SiO_3)_3^{6-}$    six-membered ring $(SiO_3)_6^{12-}$

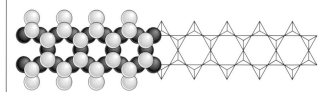

double chain $(Si_4O_{11})_n^{6n-}$

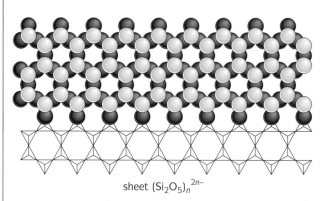

sheet $(Si_2O_5)_n^{2n-}$

● *Figure 1.10* Some structures present in silicates.

## Box 1A Ceramics

The word 'ceramics' is derived from the Greek word for earthenware, and is still used to describe a type of pottery. However, ceramics is also the name of a class of material which fits alongside metals and polymers. Ceramics are much better electrical and thermal insulators than metals; they have greater rigidity, hardness and temperature stability than polymers.

The useful properties of ceramics are:

■ extreme hardness and wear resistance
■ very high melting points
■ high resistance to chemically aggressive environments
■ high electrical resistivity
■ superconductivity (for some ceramics)

This last property, that some ceramics are superconductors, has led to their increasing use in modern society. A superconductor conducts electricity with no electrical resistance. In 1987 the Nobel Prize for physics was awarded to Alex Müller and George Bednorz for their discovery that some ceramics are superconductors. Before this, superconductivity was found only at very low temperatures of below 20 K, so any device using a superconductor had to be cooled – which made it impractical and expensive. By 1987 ceramics could be used as superconductors at operating temperatures of around 77 K, which is a much easier temperature to achieve, because relatively cheap liquid nitrogen can be used as a coolant.

The use of superconductors is still being researched but in the near future it is expected that ceramics will be used in motors, sensors, aerials and bearings. It is also predicted that the engineering ceramics market will grow rapidly as 'ceramic-fibre reinforced ceramics' are developed – these materials will replace fibre-reinforced plastics. Such materials would resist heat at temperatures of up to 1800 K and would be very tough.

All the properties of ceramics can be attributed to their giant molecular structures. The structures are very strong

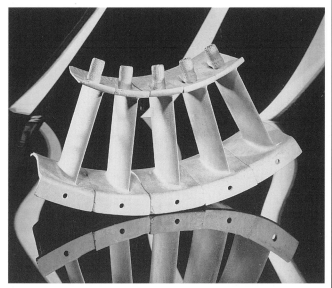

● *Figure 1.11* The ceramic exhaust outlet guide vanes in a gas turbine engine, used to power aircraft. Rolls-Royce manufacture the vanes from braided silicon carbide fibres.

because the covalent bonds form a large network, which is difficult to break up. This gives ceramics their toughness and strength. The tetrahedral shape of the basic $SiO_4$ unit means that there is little possibility of electrons passing from one molecule to another, so the electrical and thermal insulating properties of silicate-based ceramics are very good.

Although silicates form the largest group of ceramics, other materials such as magnesium oxide, MgO, and alumina, $Al_2O_3$, are also ceramics. Magnesium oxide has such a high melting point – over 2800 °C – that it is used in furnace linings as a refractory material (meaning it is resistant to heat). Alumina is more widely used, particularly for electronic substrates (the bases for printed circuit boards) and spark plugs.

| Properties | Use |
|---|---|
| thermal insulation | refractory brick linings for high temperature furnaces; usually magnesium oxide is used |
| electrical insulation | insulators in a variety of electrical goods |
| hardness and temperature stability | glass for covering solar panels |
| rigidity, hardness and temperature stability | crockery |
| rigidity, hardness, electrical and thermal insulation | parts of turbines (*figure 1.11*) and internal combustion engines |

● *Table 1.1* Properties of ceramics, and their associated uses

## Box 1B Asbestos

One of the best-known silicates is asbestos, a rock-like mineral that yields fibres when crushed. These fibres can be spun and woven into a strong material, and are also fire-resistant – asbestos can be heated to redness in a flame without apparent change. There are three main types of asbestos, white, blue and brown *(figure 1.12)*.

There are health hazards connected with asbestos dust, first suspected in about 1900. In 1920 it was accepted that high levels of this dust can cause asbestosis (thickening of the bronchioles). In 1960

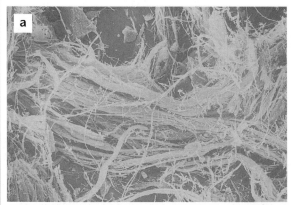

● *Figure 1.12*  Electron micrographs of
**a**  white asbestos (chrysotile)
**b**  blue asbestos (crocidolite)
**c**  brown asbestos (amosite).

published research confirmed the suspicion that blue asbestos dust can cause mesothelioma (a cancer of the lining of the chest wall).

Blue asbestos is composed of amphibole fibres, which are straight and brittle. They can puncture bronchioles and so lodge securely in lung tissue, where the damage is caused – sometimes up to 50 years later. Blue asbestos is so dangerous that it is now prohibited in most countries. White asbestos is composed of serpentine fibres, which are curly and flexible. They can be cleared from the bronchioli more easily than amphibole fibres.

The use of white asbestos is allowed but carefully controlled *(figure 1.13)*. It is used in cement products such as water pipes because the fibres are mechanically strong and so reinforce the strength of the product. It is also used in brake linings, clutches and bearings because it is resilient and resistant to the effects of hot gases, oils, water and anti-freeze solution. Workers in the asbestos industry are subject to stringent safety precautions and wear breathing apparatus so that they do not breathe in the asbestos fibres.

● *Figure 1.13*  Asbestos is disposed of with great care, and buried in landfill sites. The workers must wear protective suits and breathing masks.

### SAQ 1.9

Explain why sand is weathered very slowly.

# Aluminium

Aluminium is the most abundant metal found in the Earth's crust. It is usually present as aluminium compounds in minerals like mica, bauxite and clays. Aluminium metal is usually obtained from bauxite, which is composed mainly of aluminium oxide, $Al_2O_3$. The aluminium oxide is first separated from the other compounds in bauxite, and then undergoes electrolysis to give pure aluminium metal (the purification of aluminium by electrolysis is covered in detail in chapter 3). This process for producing aluminium was invented in 1886 and made aluminium much cheaper and easier to obtain. Before 1886 aluminium was extremely expensive. It was so rare that Napoleon III of France reserved aluminium cutlery for his special guests – ordinary guests were given cheaper silver cutlery!

## The properties of aluminium

Aluminium has typical metallic properties, including metallic bonding, a cubic close-packed structure, shiny appearance and good thermal and electrical conductivity. However, it has an unusually low density of $2700\,\text{kg}\,\text{m}^{-3}$ ($2.7\,\text{g}\,\text{cm}^{-1}$) compared with the transition metals (for instance, the density of copper is $9000\,\text{kg}\,\text{m}^{-3}$). It has other important properties too:

■ widespread availability;
■ ability to be readily fashioned or formed by most metalworking processes;
■ malleability;
■ corrosion resistance;
■ good conduction of heat and electricity.

These properties mean that aluminium has a very wide range of uses. In the UK, about $29\,400$ tonnes of aluminium are produced annually.

Aluminium is used for:

■ building – wall facings, roofing, windows, doors;
■ transport – car bumpers, radiators, engines (*figure 1.14*), container vehicle bodies, superstructure of ships, aeroplanes and tube trains;
■ packaging – mostly foil;
■ power lines.

Aluminium is, perhaps surprisingly, a highly reactive metal, and it reacts readily with oxygen and acids. This would seem to be at odds with its widespread uses, but its reactivity with air actually helps to make it so useful. The outer layer of aluminium is oxidised rapidly in air, and although this oxide layer is only about $0.01 \times 10^{-6}\,\text{m}$ thick (10 nm), it does not flake off but seals the rest of the metal below from further attack. This makes aluminium resistant to corrosion.

● *Figure 1.14* Aluminium is used in the manufacture of Indy Lights cars and as foil wrapping.

## SAQ 1.10

Write the equation showing the reaction between aluminium and oxygen to obtain the formula of the oxide coating on this metal.

This protective oxide coating can be very useful. It protects aeroplanes flying through damp air. It protects power lines – these are increasingly being made from aluminium and not copper – and pylons, which are also made from aluminium.

The protective layer is so important that it is often enhanced by an electrolytic process called

**anodising.** (Electrolysis is covered in chapter 3.) In this process the aluminium article is made the anode in an electrolyte of acids, and when current is passed, oxygen is released at the aluminium anode and the surface oxide layer is thickened to between $0.25 \times 10^{-6}$ and $150 \times 10^{-6}$ m.

Coloured anodised aluminium can be produced by adding dyes to the electrolyte.

Aluminium is also widely used in alloys because it adds strength but very little mass. An example is the alloy duralumin, which is composed of aluminium with up to 5% of copper and less than 1% of manganese, magnesium and silicon.

## Recycling aluminium

Although aluminium is found in many minerals, it is estimated that the known supply will last for less than one hundred years at the present rate of use. Recycling is one way of conserving the Earth's supply of aluminium. It is also cheaper and easier to refine recycled aluminium than to mine bauxite and extract aluminium metal by electrolysis.

Aluminium is easy to recycle and is worth more than other common recycled metals, paper and glass. Recycling aluminium cans can be a fully self-supporting and profit-making business *(figure 1.15)*.

### SAQ 1.11 _____

The life cycle of a common metal is shown in *figure 1.16*. What will happen in this life cycle if a lot of the metal is sent to the waste tip?

### Box 1C Alloys

An alloy is a mixture of a metal with one or more other metals (or sometimes other elements). One metal is used as the basis for the alloy, and is therefore present in the greatest proportion, with other components present in much smaller proportions; for example, steel is composed of iron with 0.02–2.0% carbon, with small amounts of other metals such as manganese, chromium and nickel.

Alloys are made because the properties of the main metal can be changed by adding other elements. Steel is much stronger and harder than iron, and altering the amounts of carbon added make it suitable for different purposes. Iron with 0.1% carbon is easily made into wire and is used for items like paper clips. Iron with 1% carbon is much tougher and is used to make tools and similar items.

The components of the alloy have atoms of a similar size. They are mixed together when molten, and then allowed to cool, so that the atoms of the main metal are substituted in the lattice by the atoms of the other components without much change in the structure.

● *Figure 1.15* The recycling of aluminium cans helps to save costs and conserve supplies of aluminium.

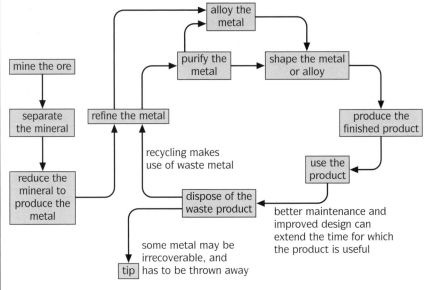

● *Figure 1.16* The life cycle of a metal.

# Copper

Approximately 90% of the world's copper comes from sulphide-containing ores such as chalcopyrite ($CuFeS_2$). Copper has the typical physical properties of transition metals. It has a lustrous appearance, is malleable and ductile, and has good thermal and electrical conductivities.

Copper is more resistant to oxidation than other members of the first row of the d-block, so it can be used as protective sheeting (*figure 1.17*), especially on roofs. Such sheeting turns green when exposed to the air owing to the formation of a layer of copper(II) carbonate, sulphate or chloride – although in some large cities a black copper(II) sulphide is formed first because of the sulphur present in pollutant gases. The main use of copper metal is in electrical cables, but it is nowadays being replaced by aluminium. However, copper is used in several important alloys such as brass and bronze. Alloy formation is typical of transition metals, and they form a wide range of alloys with each other, with other metals or with carbon.

## *Alloys of copper*

- *Brass*
  Ornaments, bullet cases — various proportions of Cu and Zn, e.g. Cu 70%, Zn 30%

- *Coinage metals*
  'Silver' coins — Cu 75%, Ni 25%
  'Copper' coins — Cu 95%, Zn 1.5%, Sn 3.5%

- *Bronze*
  Ornaments, cutlery, crockery — various proportions of Cu and Sn, e.g. Cu 90%, Sn 10%

- *Nickel silver*
  Cheap alternative to silver — various proportions of Cu, Ni and Zn, e.g. Cu 60%, Ni 30%, Zn 10%

- *Monel*
  Corrosion-resistant equipment, such as steam turbines — Ni 66%, Cu 33%, 1% mixture of Fe, Mn, Si and C

It is estimated that the Earth's reserves of copper ores will last only until the year 2030, so recycling copper is of paramount importance. This is done by electrolysis, and is discussed in chapter 3.

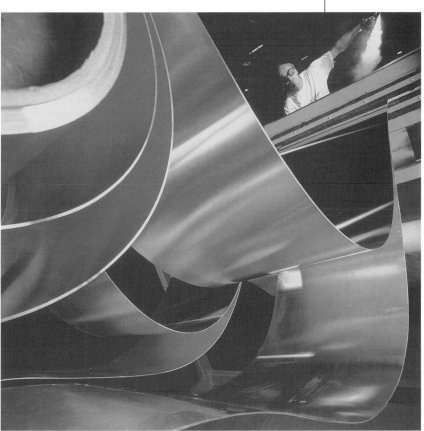

● *Figure 1.17* A stage in the manufacture of copper sheeting.

## SUMMARY

- The kinetic theory of gases assumes that gases are ideal. Ideal gases have molecules with mass but no size, and there are no internal forces between the gas molecules.

- Real gases mostly behave like ideal gases, except at high pressure or low temperature.

- Boyle's law, Charles' law and the pressure law can be combined to give the ideal gas equation, $pV = nRT$.

- $R$ is the molar gas constant. It has the approximate value $8.31\,J\,K^{-1}\,mol^{-1}$.

- The ideal gas equation can be used to determine how the pressure, volume and temperature of a gas alter when the conditions of the gas are changed. It can also be used to determine the relative molecular mass of a gas.

- Silicon(IV) oxide has a giant covalent structure, which gives it a high melting point and means it does not conduct heat and electricity well. The basic unit of this structure is the $SiO_4$ tetrahedron.

- Aluminium is a commercially important metal. It has very many uses, mostly depending on its low density combined with high strength.

- The protective oxide layer on aluminium can be thickened by anodising.

- Copper is also an important metal, usually used in alloys.

- Aluminium and copper are often recycled to conserve supplies.

## Questions

1 Explain in terms of the kinetic theory why:
   a a gas fills the container it occupies;
   b a gas exerts a pressure on the walls of its container;
   c the pressure of a fixed mass of gas increases when the temperature is raised but the volume is unchanged.

2 a Inside a television set is a cathode-ray tube with a volume of $5\,dm^3$. The pressure inside the tube is $0.10\,Pa$ at $25\,°C$. How many molecules of gas does the cathode-ray tube contain?
   b When the television set is operating, the temperature rises to $80\,°C$. What is the operating pressure of the gas in the cathode-ray tube?

3 In an industrial plant used for the production of ammonia, the ammonia is stored in a container of $100\,m^3$ at $700\,K$ and a pressure of $3 \times 10^7\,Pa$. What mass of ammonia is stored in this container?

4 Explain the corrosion resistance of aluminium in atmospheric conditions, and how this resistance is commercially increased.
   List **three** uses of aluminium, explaining the property that makes it appropriate for each use.

5 Draw the structure of the $SiO_4$ unit, and give an example of a compound in which it is found. What is the type of bonding in this unit?
   The softest mineral, talc, has a silicate structure in which the silicate ions form sheets. Predict the type of bonding found **between** the sheets, and explain why this mineral is so soft (it is the main component of talcum powder).

# Chapter two

# Redox processes: electrode potentials

## By the end of this chapter you should be able to:

1 recognise redox processes in terms of the transfer of electrons;

2 construct redox equations using the relevant half-equations;

3 establish a reactivity series for metals;

4 make up electrochemical cells using combinations of metal/metal ion half-cells, and represent them by a conventional cell statement;

5 understand how standard electrode potentials are placed in order to give the electrochemical series;

6 recognise the relationship between the reactivity series for metals and the electrochemical series;

7 use standard electrode potentials to predict if a reaction will take place, and to calculate standard cell potentials;

8 show understanding that other factors, for example kinetics, may prevent a feasible reaction from occurring;

9 describe a number of commercial batteries and cells, and understand the particular advantages and disadvantages of each;

10 explain the formation of rust and understand corrosion as an electrochemical process;

11 describe different methods to prevent rusting and explain their mode of action.

## Redox reactions

Redox reactions involve both reduction and oxidation. In this section on electrochemistry, certain redox reactions are described together with the way they are used to produce an electric current.

In electrochemistry, redox processes are defined in terms of electron transfer: **oxidation is the loss of electrons** and **reduction is the gain of electrons**.

### Reduction and oxidation

Reduction and oxidation can be defined in several ways:

| Oxidation | Reduction |
|---|---|
| gain of O by a substance | loss of O from a substance |
| loss of H from a substance | gain of H by a substance |
| loss of electrons | gain of electrons |
| increase in oxidation number | reduction in oxidation number |

For example, the half-equation

$$Zn(s) \longrightarrow Zn^{2+}(aq) + 2e^-$$

is an oxidation reaction because electrons have been lost as zinc metal becomes zinc ions. The zinc has been oxidised. Similarly, the half-equation

$$Cu^{2+}(aq) + 2e^- \longrightarrow Cu(s)$$

is a reduction because copper ions have gained electrons to become copper metal. The copper ions have been reduced.

One easy way of determining whether oxidation or reduction has taken place is to work out the oxidation numbers of the species involved. An **increase in the oxidation number** means the species has been **oxidised**. A **reduction in the oxidation number** means it has been **reduced**. In the two half-equations above, the oxidation numbers are:

$$Zn(s) \longrightarrow Zn^{2+}(aq) + 2e^-$$
oxidation number $\quad$ 0 $\qquad$ +2

the oxidation number has increased – zinc has been oxidised;

$$Cu^{2+}(aq) + 2e^- \longrightarrow Cu(s)$$
oxidation number $\quad$ +2 $\qquad\qquad$ 0

the oxidation number has decreased – copper ions have been reduced.

Reduction and oxidation can never happen in isolation but always occur together (hence the name *redox* reaction). The two half-equations shown above are added together to give the whole equation for the reaction:

$$Zn(s) + Cu^{2+}(aq) \longrightarrow Zn^{2+}(aq) + Cu(s)$$

oxidation numbers    0    +2    +2    0

For the oxidation:

increase in oxidation number = +2

For the reduction:

decrease in oxidation number = –2

## SAQ 2.1

State whether the following involve oxidation, reduction, *neither* oxidation nor reduction, or *both* oxidation and reduction.

a  $Cu^+(aq) + e^- \longrightarrow Cu(s)$

b  $2H^+(aq) + 2e^- \longrightarrow H_2(g)$

c  $Fe^{2+}(aq) \longrightarrow Fe^{3+}(aq) + e^-$

d  $Ag^+(aq) + Cl^-(aq) \longrightarrow AgCl(s)$

e  $2O^{2-}(l) \longrightarrow O_2(g) + 4e^-$

f  $Zn^{2+}(aq) + Mg(s) \longrightarrow Zn(s) + Mg^{2+}(aq)$

## SAQ 2.2

Which species is oxidised and which is reduced in the following redox equations?

a  $Zn^{2+}(aq) + Mg(s) \longrightarrow Mg^{2+}(aq) + Zn(s)$

b  $Zn(s) + Pb(NO_3)_2(aq) \longrightarrow Pb(s) + Zn(NO_3)_2(aq)$

c  $CO(g) + CuO(s) \longrightarrow Cu(s) + CO_2(g)$

# The reactivity series of metals

We have seen that metals can be oxidised; they can lose electrons to become ions:

$$M(s) \longrightarrow M^{n+}(aq) + ne^-$$

If a metal loses electrons readily to become an ion, we say it is **reactive**. For example, sodium and potassium are reactive metals – they lose their electrons readily and the chemical reactions they undergo are vigorous.

| potassium | K |
| sodium | Na |
| calcium | Ca |
| magnesium | Mg |
| aluminium | Al |
| zinc | Zn |
| iron | Fe |
| lead | Pb |
| **hydrogen** | **H** |
| copper | Cu |
| mercury | Hg |
| silver | Ag |
| platinum | Pt |
| gold | Au |

● **Table 2.1**  The reactivity series of metals (hydrogen is included in this list as a reference)

If a metal does not lose electrons readily, we say it is unreactive. For example, mercury and silver are unreactive metals – they undergo relatively few chemical reactions (think of the difference between the reactions of sodium and silver with water!)

The reactivity series of metals is a list of metals arranged in order of their reactivity (table 2.1).

Metals at the *top* of the reactivity series lose electrons more easily and form ions readily. They are known as **electropositive metals**. Sodium and potassium are examples of electropositive metals.

Metals at the *bottom* of the reactivity series lose electrons with difficulty and do not readily form ions. They are less electropositive metals.

So this series simply lists metals in order of decreasing ability to lose electrons.

# How to establish the reactivity series of metals

How can we compare the reactivity of different metals, so that they can be placed in the correct order? We can investigate reactivity by looking at the reactions of metals with:

■ water,

■ acids,

■ solutions containing other metal ions.

## The reactions of metals with water

Metals above lead in the reactivity series react with water; lead, and metals below it, do not.

The first four metals in the reactivity series (potassium, sodium, calcium and magnesium) react with cold water with decreasing reactivity, so that potassium reacts violently and magnesium reacts very slowly. These metals also react with steam with decreasing reactivity.

The next three metals (aluminium, zinc and iron) react with steam, again with decreasing reactivity, but not with cold water.

All the other metals from lead down do not react with either water or steam.

Metals react with water (and steam) by displacing hydrogen. For example, the equation for the reaction between sodium and water is:

$$2Na(s) + 2H_2O(l) \longrightarrow 2NaOH(aq) + H_2(g)$$

| sodium | water | sodium hydroxide | hydrogen |

### SAQ 2.3

Write a balanced equation, including state symbols, for the reaction of magnesium with steam.

## The reactions of metals with acids

Metals above copper in the reactivity series react with dilute acids. Copper and metals below it do not react with acids.

The metals at the top of the reactivity series – potassium, sodium and calcium – react violently with acids. The other metals react less violently.

Metals react with dilute acids by displacing hydrogen. For example, the equation for the reaction between magnesium and dilute hydrochloric acid is:

$$Mg(s) + 2HCl(aq) \longrightarrow MgCl_2(aq) + H_2(g)$$

| magnesium | hydrochloric acid | magnesium chloride | hydrogen |

Because some metals can displace hydrogen from dilute acids in this way, hydrogen itself is often inserted into the reactivity series of metals, placed above copper. All the metals above hydrogen displace hydrogen from dilute acids. Copper and the rest of the metals below hydrogen do not react with acids.

### SAQ 2.4

Write the equations for the following reactions, and identify which species are oxidised and which are reduced:

a   magnesium and sulphuric acid, $H_2SO_4$;

b   sodium and sulphuric acid;

c   sodium and hydrochloric acid.

### SAQ 2.5

Do the metals aluminium, iron and silver react with dilute hydrochloric acid? If so, write a balanced equation for the reaction.

## Displacement reactions

Reactions of metals with solutions containing other metal ions are known as **displacement reactions**.

An electropositive metal high in the reactivity series can displace a less electropositive metal from lower in the series from a solution of one of its salts.

What does this mean? Let us look at the reaction between iron filings and aqueous copper sulphate. When the iron filings are mixed with the blue aqueous copper sulphate, copper metal is formed and the solution turns from blue to very pale green – the blue copper ions are used up and pale green iron ions are formed. The equation for this reaction is:

$$Fe(s) + CuSO_4(aq) \longrightarrow FeSO_4(aq) + Cu(s)$$

|  | blue | pale green |  |

The ionic equation for this reaction is:

$$Fe(s) + Cu^{2+}(aq) \longrightarrow Fe^{2+}(aq) + Cu(s)$$

which is made up of two half-equations:

$$Fe(s) \longrightarrow Fe^{2+}(aq) + 2e^- \qquad \text{oxidation}$$
$$Cu^{2+}(aq) + 2e^- \longrightarrow Cu(s) \qquad \text{reduction}$$

Iron is higher in the reactivity series than copper, and so iron loses electrons to form iron ions, and copper ions accept these electrons to become copper atoms.

Now consider the reaction between magnesium and zinc ions. Magnesium is higher in the reactivity series and so will be oxidised to its ions. Zinc is lower in the reactivity series so its ions will be reduced to the metal. The two half-equations are:

$$Mg(s) \longrightarrow Mg^{2+}(aq) + 2e^- \quad \text{oxidation}$$
$$Zn^{2+}(aq) + 2e^- \longrightarrow Zn(s) \quad \text{reduction}$$

and so the whole ionic equation is:

$$Mg(s) + Zn^{2+}(aq) \longrightarrow Mg^{2+}(aq) + Zn(s)$$

Let us consider another possible reaction. Can zinc metal displace copper ions from solution? Zinc is higher in the reactivity series than copper, so the answer is yes:

$$Zn(s) \longrightarrow Zn^{2+}(aq) + 2e^- \quad \text{oxidation}$$
$$Cu^{2+}(aq) + 2e^- \longrightarrow Cu(s) \quad \text{reduction}$$

Notice that zinc is oxidised in this reaction, whereas in the above reaction with magnesium it is reduced. We can see that a metal can be *either* oxidised *or* reduced, depending on the other metal with which it is reacting. The **metal higher in the reactivity series** is always **oxidised**. To show that a metal can be both oxidised and reduced we write:

$$M(s) \rightleftharpoons M^{n+}(aq) + ne^-$$

The $\rightleftharpoons$ sign shows that the reaction can go both ways. It is the sign for **dynamic equilibrium**.

Lastly, consider what happens if we mix iron ions and copper metal:

$$Fe^{2+}(aq) + Cu(s) \longrightarrow \text{no reaction}$$

Iron is higher in the reactivity series than copper, so this reaction will not take place – the more reactive metal is already in the oxidised state.

## SAQ 2.6

State the equation for the reaction between zinc and aqueous lead ions.

## SAQ 2.7

Describe the two things that can be seen when copper wire is suspended in aqueous silver nitrate.

# Metals in contact with their solutions

When a metal rod is placed in a beaker containing a solution of its own metal ions, two situations can arise *(figure 2.2)*.

■ Metal atoms leave the rod and become metal ions in solution:

$$M(s) \longrightarrow M^{n+}(aq) + ne^- \quad \text{oxidation}$$

■ Metal ions leave the solution and become metal atoms on the surface of the rod:

$$M^{n+}(aq) + ne^- \longrightarrow M(s) \quad \text{reduction}$$

In the first case, the electrons that are released when the metal ions are formed stay on the rod, so the rod carries a negative charge. We say it has a **negative potential**. Zinc and magnesium are examples of metals that behave in this way.

---

## Box 2A  Dynamic equilibrium

The $\rightleftharpoons$ sign represents a dynamic equilibrium. To understand what this means, think of a sealed can of fizzy lemonade *(figure 2.1)*. Carbon dioxide gas ($CO_2(aq)$) is dissolved in the lemonade, and carbon dioxide gas ($CO_2(g)$) fills the can above the lemonade. The concentration of carbon dioxide in both the aqueous solution and the vapour is constant. But if you could watch the molecules of carbon dioxide, you would see that they are constantly moving between the lemonade and the vapour. The rate of movement of carbon dioxide from the lemonade to the vapour is the same as the rate of movement from vapour to lemonade. So although the molecules are moving, no apparent change is taking place. We represent this as

$$CO_2(aq) \rightleftharpoons CO_2(g)$$

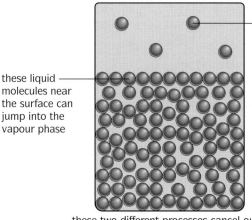

these liquid molecules near the surface can jump into the vapour phase

at the same time, vapour molecules jump into the liquid phase

these two different processes cancel out – so the overall situation remains the same

● *Figure 2.1* Dynamic equilibrium in a sealed can of fizzy lemonade.

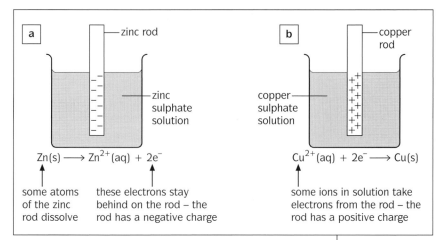

● **Figure 2.2** The behaviour of metals in contact with solutions of their ions.

In the second case, electrons are attracted out of the rod into the solution, so the rod carries a positive charge. We say it has a **positive potential**. Copper and silver are examples of metals that behave in this way.

# Electrochemical cells

We now know that a zinc rod dipping into a solution of zinc ions has a negative potential, and a copper rod dipping into a solution of copper ions has a positive potential. What happens if we connect the zinc rod and the copper rod together so that a complete circuit is made? If this is done as shown in *figure 2.3*, electrons will flow from the zinc rod to the copper rod and continue round the circuit – an electric current is produced and the lamp lights up. Such as arrangement is called an

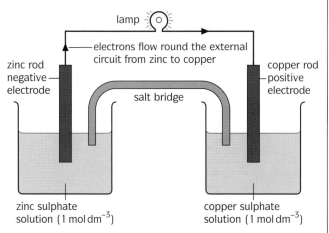

● **Figure 2.3** A simple electrochemical cell.

**electrochemical cell**. An electrochemical cell **converts chemical energy into electrical energy** using a **redox reaction**.

## *The Daniell cell*

This system using the $Zn(s)/Zn^{2+}(aq)$ and $Cu(s)/Cu^{2+}(aq)$ reactions is called the **Daniell cell**. Note that the zinc and copper rods are called the **electrodes**: the zinc rod is the **negative electrode** and the copper rod is the **positive electrode**. Each metal in contact with a solution of its ions is called a **half-cell**, and can be represented by a **half-cell equation**, which shows the electrode processes:

■ at the negative electrode

$$Zn(s) \longrightarrow Zn^{2+}(aq) + 2e^- \qquad \text{oxidation}$$

■ at the positive electrode

$$Cu^{2+}(aq) + 2e^- \longrightarrow Cu(s) \qquad \text{reduction}$$

So the ionic equation for the overall cell reaction is the two half-equations added together:

$$Zn(s) + Cu^{2+}(aq) \longrightarrow Zn^{2+}(aq) + Cu(s)$$

which is a redox reaction.

Note that the more reactive metal loses electrons and is therefore the negative electrode. The electron flow in *figure 2.3* is in a clockwise direction, from the zinc rod to the copper rod and on to the copper sulphate solution. The **salt bridge**, a strip of filter paper soaked in saturated potassium nitrate solution, completes the circuit by allowing the passage of ions from the copper sulphate solution to the zinc sulphate solution and hence to the zinc rod.

## SAQ 2.8

What happens to the mass of the zinc electrode when current is being produced by the Daniell cell?

The Daniell cell is made up of two half-cells of different potential. Electrochemical cells can be made by pairing any two half-cells of different potential so that an electric current is produced.

In *figure 2.3* a lamp shows that the electrochemical cell is producing electricity. If the lamp is replaced by a high-resistance voltmeter, a reading of +1.1 volts is obtained – this is the maximum potential difference across the cell, also called the electromotive force (e.m.f.).

As electricity is produced by the Daniell cell, the solutions are used up, and the voltage begins to drop:

| Time | Voltage |
|------|---------|
| initially | 1.1 V |
| after 5 hours | 1.063 V |
| after 12 hours | 1.052 V |
| after 23 hours | 1.002 V |
| after 24 hours | 0.00 V |

There is a continuous but slight drop in voltage as electricity is drawn from the cell, then suddenly the voltage drops to zero. We see this effect when a battery (page 25) 'runs out' – for instance, a torch battery gradually gets weaker and then fails altogether, and has to be replaced.

## Box 2B  The salt bridge

The salt bridge is an important part of the electrochemical cell. Salt bridges are often made of filter paper soaked in saturated potassium nitrate solution, or a glass U-tube filled with potassium chloride dissolved in agar jelly.

One obvious function of the salt bridge is to complete the circuit without allowing the two solutions to mix.

It has another important function too. Without it, the zinc half-cell would slowly become positively charged as electrons left it, and the copper half-cell would become negatively charged. However, when the salt bridge is in place, ions from the salt bridge are able to move in to and out of the solutions to neutralise any build-up of charge.

The salt bridge is usually made up with potassium nitrate solution because this salt does not react with other ions commonly used in electrochemical cells.

## Box 2C  The standard hydrogen electrode

The e.m.f. of the Daniell cell, +1.1 volts (V), is the maximum potential difference between the potential of the zinc half-cell and the potential of the copper half-cell. How do we find the potential of each half-cell individually? To do this we use the **standard hydrogen electrode** (s.h.e.), which is given a potential of zero volts. When it is connected to another half-cell, the e.m.f. between the s.h.e. and the second half-cell is equal to the potential of the second half-cell. We have to use a standard electrode with a potential of zero volts to calculate half-cell potentials, because there is no experimental way of measuring a potential directly.

The s.h.e. is actually the standard hydrogen half-cell *(figure 2.4)*. It consists of hydrogen gas bubbling over a platinum electrode immersed in a solution of hydrochloric acid supplying hydrogen ions. The reaction that takes place is:

$$2H^+(aq) + 2e^- \rightleftharpoons H_2(g)$$

The platinum electrode simply provides an inert metal connection between hydrogen gas, $H_2(g)$, and hydrogen ions in solution, $H^+(aq)$. The electrode is usually 'platinised', which means that the platinum metal is covered by a layer of finely divided platinum (called 'platinum black'). This increases its surface area so that it can establish an equilibrium between hydrogen gas and hydrogen ions in solution as quickly as possible.

When the s.h.e. is being used to establish the potential of a redox system, standard conditions must apply. These are:

■ The hydrogen must be at a pressure of 1 atm (101.3 kPa).
■ The concentration of the hydrogen ions must be 1 mol dm$^{-3}$.
■ The temperature must be 25°C (298 K).

(Notice that this temperature is not the same as the standard temperature of 273 K used for the gas laws.)

Under these standard conditions, the potential is defined as exactly **zero volts**. It is given the symbol $E^\ominus$, so we can say that

$$E^\ominus_{s.h.e.} = 0.00 V$$

Another way of writing this is

$$E^\ominus_{2H^+/H_2} = 0.00 V$$

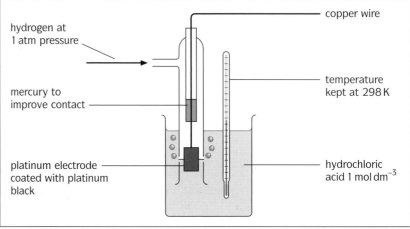

● **Figure 2.4**  The standard hydrogen electrode (s.h.e.).

## SAQ 2.9

Two different types of salt bridge are described in *box 2B*. Which do you think would be the easier to use?

## SAQ 2.10

In the Daniell cell, do nitrate ions from the salt bridge migrate into the beaker containing zinc ions or the beaker containing copper ions?

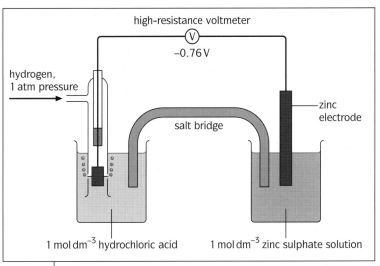

● **Figure 2.5** The arrangement required to measure the standard electrode potential of zinc.

# Standard electrode potentials

We can only measure the difference in electrode potentials between two redox systems – it is impossible to measure an electrode potential in isolation. But we can place redox systems in order of oxidising/reducing ability if we measure their electrode potential against a potential of 0.00 V, that of the standard hydrogen electrode (s.h.e.) (see *box 2C*).

To measure the electrode potential of a metal/metal ion system, for example the zinc half-cell, it is connected to the s.h.e. in the way shown in *figure 2.5*. The entire arrangement makes up an electrochemical cell composed of a hydrogen half-cell and a zinc half-cell, connected by a salt bridge. Notice that standard conditions must apply, so the zinc rod dips into a solution of $1 \, mol \, dm^{-3}$ zinc ions.

By convention, we define the e.m.f. of an electrochemical cell that is made up of two half-cells to be:

$$E^{\ominus}_{cell} = E^{\ominus}_{right\text{-}hand \, half\text{-}cell} - E^{\ominus}_{left\text{-}hand \, half\text{-}cell}$$

The s.h.e. is always used as the *left-hand* half-cell. Therefore

$$E^{\ominus}_{cell} = E^{\ominus}_{Zn^{2+}/Zn} - E^{\ominus}_{2H^+/H_2}$$

So

$$E^{\ominus}_{cell} = E^{\ominus}_{Zn^{2+}/Zn}$$

because $E^{\ominus}_{2H^+/H_2} = 0 \, V$ by definition.

When this apparatus is set up in the laboratory, we measure an electrode potential of $-0.76 \, V$. We say that

$$E^{\ominus}_{Zn^{2+}/Zn} = -0.76 \, V$$

This figure is called the **standard electrode potential** of zinc. The zinc is therefore negative compared to the s.h.e. This means that electrons flow from the zinc half-cell to the s.h.e.

The **standard electrode potential** of a metal is the potential acquired when the metal is immersed in a $1 \, mol \, dm^{-3}$ solution of its ions at a temperature of $25 \, °C$ (298 K). It has the symbol $E^{\ominus}$ and units V.

# The electrochemical series

The standard electrode potentials of other half-cells can be measured in the same way. A cell is set up consisting of the s.h.e. as one half-cell and a metal dipping into a $1 \, mol \, dm^{-3}$ solution of its ions as the other half-cell. By convention, we write each half-cell in this way:

oxidised species + electrons $\rightleftharpoons$ reduced species

For example

$$Mg^{2+}(aq) \quad + \quad 2e^- \quad \rightleftharpoons \quad Mg(s)$$

We can then tabulate all the systems in order of their standard electrode potentials to give the electrochemical series *(table 2.2)*.

The most positive $E^{\ominus}$ value is at the top. This element, fluorine (not $F^-$), is the greatest oxidising agent.

The most negative $E^{\ominus}$ value is at the bottom. This element, lithium (not $Li^+$), is the greatest reducing agent.

| Reaction | | | | $E^{\ominus}(298)/V$ |
|---|---|---|---|---|
| $F_2(g)$ | $+ 2e^-$ | $\rightleftharpoons$ | $2F^-(aq)$ | $+2.87$ |
| $Co^{3+}(aq)$ | $+ e^-$ | $\rightleftharpoons$ | $Co^{2+}(aq)$ | $+1.82$ |
| $Pb^{4+}(aq)$ | $+ 2e^-$ | $\rightleftharpoons$ | $Pb^{2+}(aq)$ | $+1.69$ |
| $Mn^{3+}(aq)$ | $+ e^-$ | $\rightleftharpoons$ | $Mn^{2+}(aq)$ | $+1.51$ |
| $Au^{3+}(aq)$ | $+ 3e^-$ | $\rightleftharpoons$ | $Au(s)$ | $+1.42$ |
| $Cl_2(aq)$ | $+ 2e^-$ | $\rightleftharpoons$ | $2Cl^-(aq)$ | $+1.36$ |
| $Br_2(aq)$ | $+ 2e^-$ | $\rightleftharpoons$ | $2Br^-(aq)$ | $+1.07$ |
| $NO_3^-(aq) + 2H^+(aq)$ | $+ e^-$ | $\rightleftharpoons$ | $NO_2(aq) + H_2O(l)$ | $+0.81$ |
| $Ag^+(aq)$ | $+ e^-$ | $\rightleftharpoons$ | $Ag(s)$ | $+0.80$ |
| $Fe^{3+}(aq)$ | $+ e^-$ | $\rightleftharpoons$ | $Fe^{2+}(aq)$ | $+0.77$ |
| $I_2(aq)$ | $+ 2e^-$ | $\rightleftharpoons$ | $2I^-(aq)$ | $+0.54$ |
| $Cu^+(aq)$ | $+ e^-$ | $\rightleftharpoons$ | $Cu(s)$ | $+0.52$ |
| $O_2(g) + 2H_2O(l)$ | $+ 4e^-$ | $\rightleftharpoons$ | $4OH^-(aq)$ | $+0.40$ |
| $Cu^{2+}(aq)$ | $+ 2e^-$ | $\rightleftharpoons$ | $Cu(s)$ | $+0.34$ |
| $SO_4^{2-}(aq) + 4H^+(aq)$ | $+ 2e^-$ | $\rightleftharpoons$ | $SO_2(aq) + 2H_2O(l)$ | $+0.17$ |
| $Cu^{2+}(aq)$ | $+ e^-$ | $\rightleftharpoons$ | $Cu^+(aq)$ | $+0.15$ |
| $Sn^{4+}(aq)$ | $+ 2e^-$ | $\rightleftharpoons$ | $Sn^{2+}(aq)$ | $+0.15$ |
| $Fe^{3+}(aq)$ | $+ 3e^-$ | $\rightleftharpoons$ | $Fe(s)$ | $+0.04$ |
| $2H^+(aq)$ | $+ 2e^-$ | $\rightleftharpoons$ | $H_2(g)$ | $0.00$ |
| $Pb^{2+}(aq)$ | $+ 2e^-$ | $\rightleftharpoons$ | $Pb(s)$ | $-0.13$ |
| $Sn^{2+}(aq)$ | $+ 2e^-$ | $\rightleftharpoons$ | $Sn(s)$ | $-0.14$ |
| $Ni^{2+}(aq)$ | $+ 2e^-$ | $\rightleftharpoons$ | $Ni(s)$ | $-0.26$ |
| $Co^{2+}(aq)$ | $+ 2e^-$ | $\rightleftharpoons$ | $Co(s)$ | $-0.28$ |
| $Cr^{3+}(aq)$ | $+ e^-$ | $\rightleftharpoons$ | $Cr^{2+}(aq)$ | $-0.41$ |
| $Fe^{2+}(aq)$ | $+ 2e^-$ | $\rightleftharpoons$ | $Fe(s)$ | $-0.44$ |
| $Cr^{3+}(aq)$ | $+ 3e^-$ | $\rightleftharpoons$ | $Cr(s)$ | $-0.74$ |
| $Zn^{2+}(aq)$ | $+ 2e^-$ | $\rightleftharpoons$ | $Zn(s)$ | $-0.76$ |
| $Cr^{2+}(aq)$ | $+ 2e^-$ | $\rightleftharpoons$ | $Cr(s)$ | $-0.90$ |
| $Al^{3+}(aq)$ | $+ 3e^-$ | $\rightleftharpoons$ | $Al(s)$ | $-1.67$ |
| $Mg^{2+}(aq)$ | $+ 2e^-$ | $\rightleftharpoons$ | $Mg(s)$ | $-2.37$ |
| $Na^+(aq)$ | $+ e^-$ | $\rightleftharpoons$ | $Na(s)$ | $-2.71$ |
| $Ca^{2+}(aq)$ | $+ 2e^-$ | $\rightleftharpoons$ | $Ca(s)$ | $-2.84$ |
| $K^+(aq)$ | $+ e^-$ | $\rightleftharpoons$ | $K(s)$ | $-2.93$ |
| $Li^+(aq)$ | $+ e^-$ | $\rightleftharpoons$ | $Li(s)$ | $-3.04$ |

● **Table 2.2** Standard electrode potentials, making the electrochemical series

Notice that the half-cell equation is an equilibrium reaction – it can go either way. The reaction can be a reduction or an oxidation depending on the potential of the other half-cell.

The metals in the electrochemical series are in mostly the reversed order of the metals in the reactivity series. This is no surprise; the most reactive metals at the top of the reactivity series lose electrons easily, so have the most negative $E^{\ominus}$ values and are at the bottom of the electrochemical series.

There is one exception to this reversed order in the electrochemical series – can you spot it?

There is a general rule for reactions in solution: an element lower in the electrochemical series will displace an element higher in the series.

There are two things to remember about the electrochemical series:

■ It gives no information about the *rate* of a reaction. Find sodium and calcium in the electrochemical series. Sodium is above calcium, so is less reactive. Yet sodium reacts much more vigorously than calcium with water. The electrochemical series cannot give us this information.

■ The electrochemical series only refers to *standard conditions*. Changes in temperature, pressure and concentration will affect $E^{\ominus}$ values.

The electrochemical series cannot give other important pieces of information either. If you look up aluminium in the electrochemical series you will find it is lower than hydrogen – aluminium should theoretically displace hydrogen from water. However, a piece of aluminium dropped into a beaker of water does not react at all (luckily for all those aeroplanes flying through clouds!). Why? The series does not tell us that aluminium is covered by a thin film of aluminium oxide, which prevents the metal reacting with water.

# Making electrochemical cells: the standard cell potential

We have already seen how a zinc half-cell and a copper half-cell can be combined to make a Daniell cell. We can calculate the **standard cell potential,**

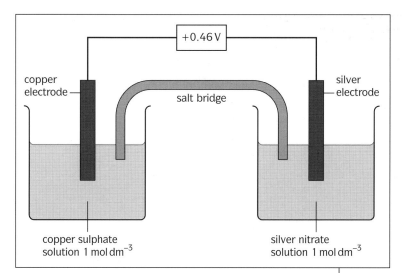

● **Figure 2.6** The electrochemical cell formed by connecting copper and silver half-cells.

$E^{\ominus}_{cell}$, from the standard electrode potentials of the half-cells in this way:

$$E^{\ominus}_{cell} = E^{\ominus}_{\text{right-hand half-cell}} - E^{\ominus}_{\text{left-hand half-cell}}$$

The left-hand cell is conventionally the oxidising half-cell – the one lower in the electrochemical series with the more negative $E^{\ominus}$ value. So

$$E^{\ominus}_{cell} = E^{\ominus}_{Cu^{2+}/Cu} - E^{\ominus}_{Zn^{2+}/Zn}$$
$$= +0.34 - (-0.76)\,V$$
$$= +1.1\,V$$

This is called the standard cell potential because standard conditions are operating – each solution is at $1\,mol\,dm^{-3}$ concentration at a temperature of 298 K. If the conditions are not standard, then the potential calculated is called the cell potential, and given the symbol $E$.

Notice that the $E^{\ominus}$ value is positive for this cell. This tells us that electrons travel round the external circuit from the left-hand cell $(Zn(s) \longrightarrow Zn^{2+}(aq) + 2e^{-})$ to the right-hand cell $(Cu^{2+}(aq) + 2e^{-} \longrightarrow Cu(s))$. So the zinc is the negative electrode and the copper is the positive electrode. The sign of $E^{\ominus}$ tells us the polarity of the right-hand half-cell.

Another example of combining half-cells to make an electrochemical cell is shown in *figure 2.6*. Look at the $E^{\ominus}$ values for copper and silver – the copper has the more negative potential, so copper is the more reactive metal and the copper half-cell

is placed on the left-hand side. Now we can calculate the standard cell potential:

$$E^{\ominus}_{cell} = E^{\ominus}_{\text{right-hand half-cell}} - E^{\ominus}_{\text{left-hand half-cell}}$$
$$= E^{\ominus}_{Ag^{+}/Ag} - E^{\ominus}_{Cu^{2+}/Cu}$$
$$= +0.80 - (+0.34)\,V$$
$$= +0.46\,V$$

Notice that, in both these cases, the e.m.f. of the cell is positive. This is true for all spontaneous processes. **A spontaneous change has a positive e.m.f.** A change that will *not* occur spontaneously has a *negative* e.m.f.

### SAQ 2.11

A cell is made up of magnesium and zinc half-cells.

**a** Which is the more reactive metal, magnesium or zinc?

**b** Sketch a diagram of the cell.

**c** Calculate the standard cell potential of this cell.

**d** State which is the positive electrode.

**e** Indicate the direction of electron flow in the external circuit.

## Cell statements

Cell statements are a convenient shorthand way of representing an electrochemical cell, without having to draw a diagram. The cell statement for the Daniell cell is shown in *figure 2.7*. The continuous vertical lines represent a **phase boundary**, or change in state – in this case between a solid metal and a solution. The broken vertical lines represent a barrier, the salt bridge, which does not allow mixing of the solutions but does allow electricity to pass.

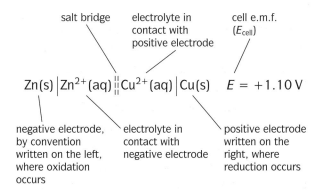

● **Figure 2.7** The cell statement for the Daniell cell.

Write down the cell statement for a cell made up of a zinc half-cell and a silver half-cell. Calculate the e.m.f. (standard cell potential) of this cell.

# What is the cell reaction?

The cell reaction tells us the direction in which a reaction proceeds if we allow electricity to flow through the circuit.

The cell statement conventionally shows the more reactive metal on the left-hand side; this metal releases electrons. The metal on the right is less reactive; the ions accept electrons to become metal atoms. The two half-reactions are added together to give the cell reaction *(figure 2.8)*. **The cell reaction takes place as written in the cell statement.**

When the two electrode reactions are added together to give the cell reaction, the number of electrons transferred in each half-reaction must be the same. So for this cell

$$Cu(s) \mid Cu^{2+}(aq) \parallel Ag^+(aq) \mid Ag(s)$$

The two half-reactions are:

$$Cu(s) \longrightarrow Cu^{2+}(aq) + 2e^-$$

and

$$Ag^+(aq) + e^- \longrightarrow Ag(s)$$

The latter must be doubled so the number of electrons in each half-reaction is equal. Therefore, the cell reaction is

$$Cu(s) + 2Ag^+(aq) \longrightarrow Cu^{2+}(aq) + 2Ag(s)$$

---

Cell statement

$$Ni(s) \mid Ni^{2+}(aq) \parallel Cu^{2+}(aq) \mid Cu(s)$$

so $Ni(s) \rightarrow Ni^{2+}(aq)$ and $Cu^{2+}(aq) \rightarrow Cu(s)$

---

$$Ni(s) \rightarrow Ni^{2+}(aq) + 2e^-$$
$$Cu^{2+}(aq) + 2e^- \rightarrow Cu(s)$$
$$\overline{Ni(s) + Cu^{2+}(aq) \rightarrow Ni^{2+}(aq) + Cu(s)}$$

● *Figure 2.8* Deducing the cell reaction from the cell statement.

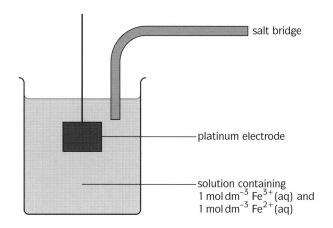

● *Figure 2.9* The apparatus used to form a half-cell from two solutions of ions.

## *Measuring $E^\ominus$ values of half-cells involving no metals*

Some redox systems such as $Fe^{3+}(aq)/Fe^{2+}(aq)$ do not involve solid metals, but only solutions. In such cases, a platinum electrode is used as the electrical connection *(figure 2.9)*.

## *Predicting which reaction will take place*

If two of the systems shown in the electrochemical series are linked, for example in a cell, we can predict what will happen. The system which is lower in the series will lose electrons, and the system which is higher in the series will gain electrons.

So, consider linking these two systems:

$$Fe^{2+}(aq)/Fe(s) \qquad E^\ominus = -0.44\,V$$
$$Co^{2+}(aq)/Co(s) \qquad E^\ominus = -0.28\,V$$

The first system is lower in the electrochemical series, as it has the more negative value of $E^\ominus$. Therefore, when the two systems are linked, this system will lose electrons:

$$Fe(s) \longrightarrow Fe^{2+}(aq) + 2e^-$$

and the system higher in the electrochemical series will gain electrons:

$$Co^{2+}(aq) + 2e^- \longrightarrow Co(s)$$

Now consider the following two electrode systems:

$$I_2(aq)/2I^-(aq) \qquad E^{\ominus} = +0.54\,V$$
$$Fe^{3+}(aq)/Fe^{2+}(aq) \qquad E^{\ominus} = +0.77\,V$$

If a cell is made up of these two systems, then the following half-cell reactions must occur:

lower in series $\quad 2I^-(aq) \longrightarrow I_2(aq) + 2e^-$
higher in series $\quad Fe^{3+}(aq) + e^- \longrightarrow Fe^{2+}(aq)$

But when the complete reaction is written, the electron gain and loss must be **equal** – so the second equation must be multiplied throughout by 2, giving

$$2Fe^{3+}(aq) + 2I^-(aq) \longrightarrow 2Fe^{2+}(aq) + I_2(aq)$$

## SAQ 2.13 _____

Some electrochemical cells are made by linking the following systems. Write down the correct half-cell equations, and the cell equation, for each example.

**a** $Co^{2+}(aq)/Co(s)$ and $Ni^{2+}(aq)/Ni(s)$.

**b** $Fe^{3+}(aq)/Fe^{2+}(aq)$ and $Ag^+(aq)/Ag(s)$.

**c** $Cr^{3+}(aq)/Cr(s)$ and $Fe^{2+}(aq)/Fe(s)$.

## SAQ 2.14 _____

Would you expect the $E^{\ominus}$ values of the electrochemical cells in SAQ 2.13 to be positive or negative?

# Batteries and commercial cells

Electrochemical cells are used widely in everyday life – in radios, battery-operated razors, smoke alarms, toys, torches, digital watches, motor vehicles and many other products. One of the most recently developed electrochemical cells is a sodium–sulphur battery, which is used to power a Ford Escort Ecostar police van. This van has a top speed of 70 m.p.h. and similar acceleration to a petrol or diesel Escort van, but is more environmentally friendly. It has another advantage too – there is no engine noise, which is especially useful in police work!

The difference between a battery and a cell is that a battery consists of two or more cells joined together. There are two sorts of battery – primary

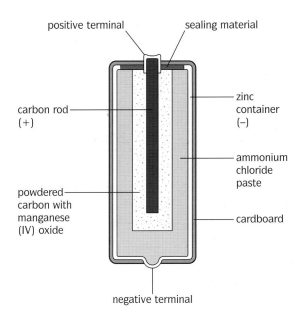

● **Figure 2.10**  The dry cell.

batteries, which cannot be recharged but are thrown away when they run down, and secondary batteries, which can be recharged.

## *The dry cell*

One of the most common and most widely used primary batteries is the carbon–zinc dry cell *(figure 2.10)*. It is usually called a battery, but in fact it is a cell. It has an e.m.f. of about 1.5 V, which drops gradually as the cell is used, but more rapidly at the very end of its life. This type of cell is cheap, portable and easy to use but has a relatively short life and has to be thrown away when it is used up. Notice that a paste of ammonium chloride is used, as a solution would prove far too messy!

The simplified electrode reactions are:

at the negative electrode
$$Zn(s) \longrightarrow Zn^{2+}(aq) + 2e^-$$
at the positive electrode
$$2NH_4^+(aq) + 2e^- \longrightarrow 2NH_3(g) + H_2(g)$$
overall cell reaction
$$Zn(s) + 2NH_4^+(aq)$$
$$\longrightarrow Zn^{2+}(aq) + 2NH_3(g) + H_2(g)$$

The hydrogen gas produced at the positive electrode is removed by reaction with the manganese(IV) oxide:

$$H_2(g) + 2MnO_2(s) \longrightarrow Mn_2O_3(s) + H_2O(l)$$

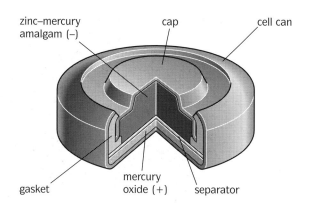

● *Figure 2.11* The mercury oxide–zinc button cell.

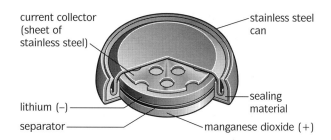

● *Figure 2.12* The lithium–manganese dioxide button cell.

## Button cells

Button cells are used in calculators, digital watches, hearing aids, camera exposure meters and general electronic instrumentation. They have an e.m.f. of about 1.5 V and last for about one year.

There are three types of button cells: a mercury oxide–zinc cell, a silver oxide–zinc cell and a zinc–air cell. The most widely used is the mercury oxide–zinc cell *(figure 2.11)*. These cells are widely used because they are small and convenient, and because the voltage does not drop at all until very near the end of a cell's life.

In the mercury oxide–zinc cell, the electrode reactions are as follows.

At the negative electrode:
$$Zn(s) + 2OH^-(aq) \longrightarrow ZnO(s) + H_2O(l) + 2e^-$$
At the positive electrode:
$$HgO(s) + H_2O(l) + 2e^- \longrightarrow Hg(l) + 2OH^-(aq)$$
Overall cell reaction:
$$Zn(s) + HgO(s) \longrightarrow ZnO(s) + Hg(l)$$

The mercury produced is deposited in the cathode during discharge and remains trapped there. It does not short-circuit the cell because a special separator material prevents this, but this mercury can prove a problem when disposing of the cell. Mercury is a heavy metal that is toxic and difficult to disperse.

## The lithium cell

This cell is a particular type of button cell with a much higher voltage of 3 V *(figure 2.12)*. It can be produced in a very small size, and is used in heart pacemakers because a high-energy miniature battery

is necessary in this situation. It is more expensive than other button cells, but is being increasingly used in watches and other small electrical goods.

The lithium cell is the most recent type of cell to be developed. Lithium reacts vigorously with water. This meant that non-aqueous pastes had to be developed, and also new production techniques for the cell in a completely dry atmosphere.

At the negative electrode:
$$Li(s) \longrightarrow Li^+(s) + e^-$$
At the positive electrode:
$$Li^+(s) + MnO_2(s) + e^- \longrightarrow LiMnO_2(s)$$
Overall cell reaction:
$$Li(s) + MnO_2(s) \longrightarrow LiMnO_2(s)$$

## The lead–acid battery

Lead–acid batteries are the batteries found in almost all cars and other motor vehicles *(figure 2.13)*. They are made up of secondary cells, and so

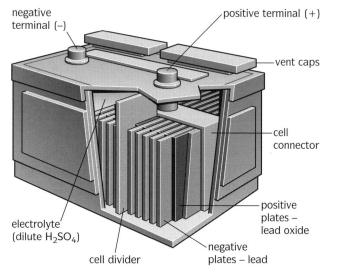

● *Figure 2.13* A typical lead–acid car battery.

can be recharged. A typical car battery consists of six cells, each with an e.m.f. of 2 V, so the total e.m.f. is 12 V.

In each cell there are two types of plates, which act as the electrodes, separated from each other and immersed in dilute sulphuric acid of density $1.25\,g\,cm^{-3}$. One type of plate is lead, and these are the negative electrodes. The other type of plate is lead coated with lead(IV) oxide, $PbO_2$, and these are the positive electrodes.

At the negative electrodes:

$$Pb(s) + SO_4^{2-}(aq) \rightleftharpoons PbSO_4(s) + 2e^-$$

At the positive electrodes:

$$PbO_2(s) + SO_4^{2-}(aq) + 4H^+(aq) + 2e^-$$
$$\rightleftharpoons PbSO_4(s) + 2H_2O(l)$$

When current is being drawn from this battery to work the car lights, radio, etc., both these reactions lie to the right and $PbSO_4$ is made by both processes. When the car moves, the alternator generates an electric current, which passes into the battery, and consequently both the reactions above go to the left. In other words, the $PbSO_4$ made when current is drawn from the cell is decomposed again when the car is running. This is how the cell is recharged. However, with time, the sulphuric acid needs replacing because it slowly decomposes, and if the battery is left in the discharged state for too long (if the car lights have been left on, for example) then so much $PbSO_4$ builds up on the plates that it cannot be removed. In this case the battery must be thrown away.

### The fuel cell

Fuel cells are primary cells, but the substances that produce electricity are constantly replaced, so theoretically the cell never runs out or needs replacing. The cell consists of porous carbon electrodes in contact with an alkali solution, and the gases hydrogen and oxygen (*figure 2.14*).

At the negative electrode:

$$H_2(g) + 2OH^-(aq) \longrightarrow 2H_2O(l) + 2e^-$$

At the positive electrode:

$$O_2(g) + 2H_2O(l) + 4e^- \longrightarrow 4OH^-(aq)$$

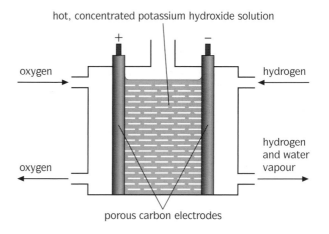

● *Figure 2.14* A simple fuel cell.

So that the cell reaction is:

$$2H_2(g) + O_2(g) \longrightarrow 2H_2O(l)$$

Fuel cells are thought to be the most promising cell of the future, as they are cheap, convenient and pollution-free (their only product is water). They were used on the American Gemini space probes and the Apollo moon vehicles. Some experimental types of fuel cell have been used to fuel cars, which is highly desirable if pollution is to be reduced, but they are too expensive and inconvenient to be commonly available. Cars driven by such cells can reach a top speed of 75 m.p.h.

# The rusting of iron

It is well known that iron rusts easily. It is estimated that this corrosion costs the UK alone over one billion pounds every year, so controlling this rusting is important. Rust is a hydrated iron(III) oxide with the general formula $Fe_2O_3.xH_2O$, where $x$ is a variable number.

Rusting can only occur when oxygen and water are both present. It is an electrochemical process involving two redox half-equations. The corrosion begins at a site on the surface of the iron where there are imperfections or impurities (*figure 2.15*), and the iron is oxidised to $Fe^{2+}$ ions:

$$Fe(s) \longrightarrow Fe^{2+}(aq) + 2e^- \qquad E^{\ominus} = -0.44\,V$$

The iron is acting as a negative terminal. The electrons released travel through the iron to an area

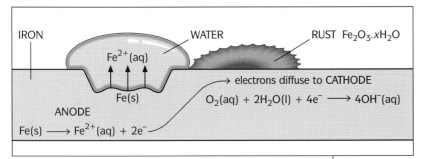

● *Figure 2.15* How iron rusts.

where it is in contact with oxygen, and this forms the positive terminal:

$$O_2(aq) + 2H_2O(l) + 4e^- \longrightarrow 4OH^-(aq)$$
$$E^\ominus = +1.23\,V$$

So at the positive terminal hydroxide ions are formed. The next stage is that the $Fe^{2+}$ and $OH^-$ ions form insoluble iron(II) hydroxide:

$$Fe^{2+}(aq) + 2OH^-(aq) \longrightarrow Fe(OH)_2(s)$$

which is readily oxidised to give iron(III) hydroxide, $Fe(OH)_3$. This partially dehydrates to give rust, which has the general formula $Fe_2O_3.xH_2O$.

Notice that the most negative electrode potential is for the oxidation of iron, as you would expect if the entire reaction is spontaneous.

## *Preventing rust on iron*

There are three different ways of preventing rust.

### Coating the iron

One method is to coat the iron with a layer of paint, oil, grease or tin; this simply prevents the oxygen and water from coming into contact with the iron. The covering layer must not be scratched if it is to be effective – any uncovered metal will rust.

In fact, if the iron is coated in tin, then scratching the tin layer actually accelerates the rusting process. This is because iron is lower in the electrochemical series than tin. When the two metals are in contact, iron has the greater tendency to form ions:

$$Fe(s) \longrightarrow Fe^{2+}(aq) + 2e^-$$

Any tin ions are reduced to atoms:

$$Sn^{2+}(aq) + 2e^- \longrightarrow Sn(s)$$

The production of $Fe^{2+}$ ions is, of course, the first stage in the rusting process – so any dissolved tin on the surface of the iron accelerates corrosion.

## Cathodic protection

A very effective way of preventing rust is to coat the iron with zinc. This process is called **galvanising**, and it works because zinc is higher in the electrochemical series than iron. Therefore zinc has the greater tendency to form ions. So if the rusting process begins, and $Fe^{2+}$ ions are formed, then:

$$Zn(s) \longrightarrow Zn^{2+}(aq) + 2e^- \quad \text{negative terminal}$$

and

$$Fe^{2+}(aq) + 2e^- \longrightarrow Fe(s) \quad \text{positive terminal}$$

The iron must act as the positive terminal, and the $Fe^{2+}$ ions are reduced back to Fe atoms – rusting cannot progress. This method of protection works even if the zinc layer is scratched.

This method is called **cathodic protection** because the positive terminal was routinely called the cathode, and the presence of the zinc protects (encourages) the reaction at this electrode.

Another metal more reactive than iron which works by cathodic protection is magnesium. This is often used to prevent corrosion in ships and on oil-rigs. A large block of magnesium is bolted to the hull of the ship or the oil-rig below the water line. The magnesium block gradually goes into solution and prevents corrosion of the iron. This is often called a **sacrificial anode**. Blocks of zinc can also be used instead of magnesium. The sacrificial metal can be replaced when it has been completely reacted away.

### SAQ 2.15

What are the reactions at the positive terminal and the negative terminal when magnesium is used to prevent rust?

## Alloying

Alloying the iron also helps to prevent corrosion – the iron is usually alloyed with nickel, chromium or carbon. The presence of another element helps to prevent the released electrons from travelling through the iron to combine with oxygen.

# SUMMARY

■ Redox reactions involve a transfer of electrons.

■ A reactivity series for metals can be established using the reactions of metals with water, with acids and with each other. This series places metals in decreasing order of reactivity.

■ An electrochemical cell is made up of two half-cells with different potentials, connected by a salt bridge. The half-cells are often metal rods dipping into a solution of their ions. Such a cell converts chemical energy into electrical energy using a redox reaction.

■ An electrode potential can only be measured against another potential. The standard used for such measurements is the standard hydrogen electrode, which has been given a standard electrode potential of 0.00 V.

■ The electrochemical series places elements in order of their power as oxidising agents. This means that $E^{\ominus}$ values decrease going down the electrochemical series.

■ A cell statement is a convenient and conventional way to represent a cell. The cell reaction takes place as written in the cell statement, and is composed of two half-reactions.

■ Electrochemical cells are used commercially in many different ways, including the dry cell, the fuel cell and the lead–acid battery.

■ Rusting of iron is an electrochemical process. This corrosion can be prevented by different methods such as galvanising.

## Questions

1 a Calculate $E^{\ominus}$ values for the cells made from these standard half-cells:
   (i) $Mg^{2+}(aq)/Mg(s)$ and $Pb^{2+}(aq)/Pb(s)$;
   (ii) $Fe^{2+}(aq)/Fe(s)$ and $Ni^{2+}(aq)/Ni(s)$.
  b Write an overall equation for the reaction occurring in each cell.

2 Until recently, most dental fillings were a mixture of silver, copper, tin and mercury. A person with such a filling can feel pain if they bite on aluminium foil. Look up the standard electrode potentials for aluminium, silver, copper, tin and mercury, and explain why this pain occurs. [NB: Saliva can act as an electrolyte.]

3 Car bodies are made of steel, an alloy of iron. However, they are still susceptible to rust. In order to help prevent this corrosion, the electrical circuit of the car generally has a negative earth (in other words, the steel body is connected to the negative terminal of the car battery). How does this help to prevent rusting?

# Redox processes: electrolysis

## What is electrolysis?

In chapter 2 we looked at the production of electricity by a chemical reaction. Now we will look at the reverse process – an electric current bringing about a chemical reaction. Electrolysis is the general term used for **chemical change** in liquids and solutions **brought about by an electric current**.

## The electrolysis of molten salts

Sodium chloride is a solid salt, made up of sodium ions and chloride ions, that does not conduct electricity. However, if it is molten (or fused) then the ions are dissociated and move about freely. If a potential difference is then applied across the fused salt by placing electrodes in it, the positive sodium ions move towards the negative electrode and the

negative chloride ions move towards the positive electrode (*figure 3.1*).

The molten sodium chloride is called the **electrolyte**. An electrolyte can also be a solution of a salt, such as sodium chloride dissolved in water. The definition of an electrolyte is that it contains free ions and is **chemically changed by the passage of electricity**. The negative electrode is called the **cathode**, and the positive electrode is called the **anode**.

What happens during the electrolysis of molten sodium chloride? The positive ions travel to the cathode and are reduced as they gain electrons:

$$Na^+(l) + e^- \longrightarrow Na(s)$$

Sodium metal is therefore deposited at the cathode.

The negative ions travel to the anode and are oxidised as they lose electrons:

$$2Cl^-(l) \longrightarrow Cl_2(g) + 2e^-$$

Chlorine gas is therefore given off at the anode.

We say that sodium ions and chloride ions have been discharged (or that sodium and chlorine have been **liberated**) at the cathode and anode respectively. **Reduction** always takes place at the **cathode** (negative electrode). **Oxidation** always takes place at the **anode** (positive electrode).

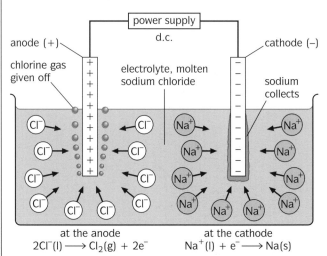

at the anode
$$2Cl^-(l) \longrightarrow Cl_2(g) + 2e^-$$

at the cathode
$$Na^+(l) + e^- \longrightarrow Na(s)$$

● *Figure 3.1* The electrolysis of molten sodium chloride.

# The electrolysis of aqueous salts

The electrolysis of aqueous sodium chloride (sodium chloride dissolved in water) is more complicated than the electrolysis of molten sodium chloride. This is because there are not only sodium ions and chloride ions, but water molecules as well. In this electrolysis, chlorine is liberated at the anode just like for fused sodium chloride, but hydrogen gas is liberated at the cathode and not sodium:

at the cathode

$$2H_2O(l) + 2e^- \longrightarrow H_2(g) + 2OH^-(aq)$$

at the anode

$$2Cl^-(aq) \longrightarrow Cl_2(g) + 2e^-$$

In this case, water molecules have been discharged at the cathode instead of sodium ions.

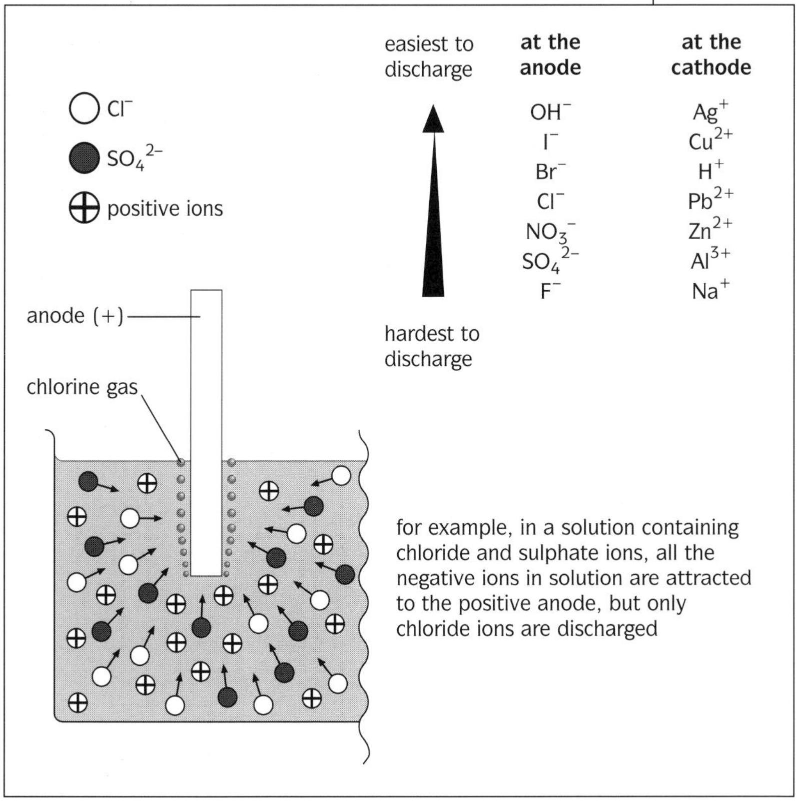

In the electrolysis of aqueous potassium nitrate, $KNO_3$, water molecules are discharged at both the cathode and the anode:

at the cathode

$$4H_2O(l) + 4e^- \longrightarrow 2H_2(g) + 4OH^-(aq)$$

at the anode

$$2H_2O(l) \longrightarrow O_2(g) + 4H^+(aq) + 4e^-$$

How can we predict which ions or molecules will be discharged during the electrolysis of aqueous solutions? Well, only *one* ion or molecule in an aqueous solution is discharged at each electrode, no matter how many ions are present. We find that some ions are discharged more easily than others, as shown in *figure 3.2* – this is called **selective discharge**.

This is only an approximate order of discharge and can be changed if the concentrations of the ions are altered.

## *Example of selective discharge at the cathode*

In an aqueous solution containing magnesium ions and iron(II) ions, which will be discharged? Look at the standard electrode potential for each metal:

$$E^{\ominus}_{Mg^{2+}/Mg} = -2.37\,V$$
$$E^{\ominus}_{Fe^{2+}/Fe} = -0.44\,V$$

Iron is the less reactive metal and has the more positive standard electrode potential, so iron ions are discharged:

$$Fe^{2+}(aq) + 2e^- \longrightarrow Fe(s)$$

## *Example of selective discharge at the anode*

In an aqueous solution containing bromide ions and chloride ions, which will be discharged? Once again, look at the standard electrode potential for each element:

$$E^{\ominus}_{Br_2/2Br^-} = +1.07\,V$$
$$E^{\ominus}_{Cl_2/2Cl^-} = +1.36\,V$$

| | easiest to discharge | at the anode | at the cathode |
|---|---|---|---|
| ◯ $Cl^-$ | | $OH^-$ | $Ag^+$ |
| ⬤ $SO_4^{2-}$ | | $I^-$ | $Cu^{2+}$ |
| ⊕ positive ions | | $Br^-$ | $H^+$ |
| | | $Cl^-$ | $Pb^{2+}$ |
| | | $NO_3^-$ | $Zn^{2+}$ |
| | | $SO_4^{2-}$ | $Al^{3+}$ |
| | hardest to discharge | $F^-$ | $Na^+$ |

anode (+)
chlorine gas

for example, in a solution containing chloride and sulphate ions, all the negative ions in solution are attracted to the positive anode, but only chloride ions are discharged

● **Figure 3.2** Selective discharge.

Bromine is the less reactive halogen and has the more negative standard electrode potential, so bromine ions are discharged:

$$2Br^-(aq) \longrightarrow Br_2(l) + 2e^-$$

## SAQ 3.2

An aqueous solution of zinc sulphate and copper sulphate is electrolysed. Which ion is discharged at the cathode?

# The electrolysis of copper(II) sulphate solution

Aqueous copper sulphate can undergo electrolysis with copper electrodes or with inert electrodes such as platinum. The results provide another example of how the products of electrolysis depend on the selective discharge of ions or molecules.

In copper sulphate solution, the possible ions or molecules to be discharged are $Cu^{2+}$, $SO_4^{2-}$ and $H_2O$.

- **With inert platinum electrodes**
  In this case $H_2O$ molecules and $Cu^{2+}$ ions are discharged:

  at the cathode
  $$Cu^{2+}(aq) + 2e^- \longrightarrow Cu(s)$$

  at the anode
  $$2H_2O(l) \longrightarrow 4H^+(aq) + O_2(g) + 4e^-$$

The copper metal produced at the cathode clings to the electrode, so that it becomes covered with a layer of copper. This is the basis of **electroplating**.

- **With copper electrodes**
  In this case copper metal and copper ions are discharged. Copper metal is discharged at the anode as copper has a more negative electrode potential than water:

  at the cathode
  $$Cu^{2+}(aq) + 2e^- \longrightarrow Cu(s)$$

  at the anode
  $$Cu(s) \longrightarrow Cu^{2+}(aq) + 2e^-$$

These equations show us that the copper anode will gradually be worn away during electrolysis,

## Box 3A Electroplating

Electroplating is often used in industry to give an even coating of metal over an object. For instance, cutlery and other objects may be silver-plated, decorative parts of cars and bicycle handlebars are often chromium-plated, and copper plating is popular for decorative items *(figure 3.3)*.

The object to be plated is made the cathode in an electrolysis bath. The electrolyte contains aqueous metal ions – silver ions for silver plating, copper ions for copper plating. When current flows through the electrolysis bath, the metal ions travel to the cathode and are deposited in an equal amount over all the electrode, which is the object to be plated. The longer and greater the current that flows, the more metal is deposited on the cathode and therefore the thicker the plate.

● *Figure 3.3* Metal plating is often used for decorative effect.

and the copper cathode will become coated with more copper. The increase in mass of the cathode is equal to the decrease in mass of the anode.

## SAQ 3.3

These questions refer to the electrolysis of aqueous copper sulphate.

a   Why does the blue colour of copper(II) sulphate solution gradually disappear when it undergoes electrolysis with inert electrodes?

b   When the solution is almost colourless, bubbles appear at the cathode. What are they, and why do they appear?

c   When does the electrolysis of aqueous copper sulphate stop?

# Faraday's laws of electrolysis

Michael Faraday was the first person to investigate electrolysis in a quantitative way. He formulated two laws.

**Faraday's first law:** the mass of a substance discharged at an electrode is proportional to the charge passed.

Charge is given the symbol $Q$ and can be calculated by measuring the current ($I$) and the time ($t$):

$$Q = It$$

Units: charge $Q$ is measured in coulombs (C); current $I$ is measured in amperes (A); time $t$ is measured in seconds (s).

The charge corresponds to a definite number of electrons, because the charge is caused by the flow of electrons and each electron has a charge $e$ of magnitude $1.602 \times 10^{-19}$ C. The charge on one mole of electrons is the Faraday constant, $F$:

$$F = Le$$

where $L$ is the Avogadro constant, $6.022 \times 10^{23}\,\text{mol}^{-1}$. So

$$F = (1.602 \times 10^{-19}\,\text{C}) \times (6.022 \times 10^{23}\,\text{mol}^{-1})$$
$$= 96\,470\,\text{C}\,\text{mol}^{-1}$$

The value for the Faraday constant depends on the number of significant figures used for $e$ and $L$ – it is often taken to be $96\,500\,\text{C}\,\text{mol}^{-1}$.

It follows that:

$$\frac{\text{number of moles of electrons}}{\text{passed during electrolysis}} = \frac{Q}{F}$$

**Faraday's second law:** in order to liberate 1 mole of a substance, a whole number of moles of electrons must be supplied.

For instance, the charge needed to discharge 1 mole of zinc ions is equal to 2 moles of electrons. This tells us that zinc ions are $Zn^{2+}$.

Now consider the following example. After a current of 1.47 A was passed through aqueous copper sulphate for 8 minutes 45 seconds, a mass of 0.254 g of copper was collected. What is the charge on the copper ion? [$M_r$ for copper is 63.5.]

Using the equation for charge

$$Q = It$$

we can substitute the values of $I$ and $t$, i.e. current $I = 1.47$ A and time $t = 8$ minutes 45 seconds = 525 s. Therefore

$$Q = 1.47 \times 525$$
$$= 772\,\text{C}$$

---

## Box 3B  Michael Faraday

Michael Faraday was born in 1791. He became involved in science at the age of 21 after attending a lecture by the famous chemist Humphrey Davy and sending Davy his lecture notes. Davy was so impressed he appointed Faraday as his assistant at the Royal Institution in London. This was a great advancement for Faraday, who had been apprenticed to a bookbinder at the age of 14 and had received very little education.

Faraday made many discoveries; for example, he established the correct empirical formula of rubber, $C_5H_8$; he isolated benzene; he succeeded in liquefying chlorine; and he discovered two new chlorides of carbon. In the field of electromagnetism he introduced the principle of induction, and expressed the electric current induced in a wire by the number of magnetic field lines that are cut by the wire (this concept was rejected by many scientists of the time). Another of his discoveries – that an intense magnetic field can rotate the plane of polarised light – is called the Faraday effect.

Faraday formulated his laws of electrolysis in 1834, continuing the initial work of Davy, who showed in 1807 that sodium and potassium can be extracted from their compounds by an electric current.

Faraday was appointed Director of the laboratory at the Royal Institution in 1825. He died in 1867.

● *Figure 3.4* Michael Faraday.

$$\text{number of moles of electrons} = \frac{Q}{F}$$

$$= \frac{772}{96\,500}$$

$$= 8.0 \times 10^{-3}\,\text{mol}$$

Then

number of moles of copper collected

$$= \frac{\text{mass in grams}}{\text{molar mass}}$$

$$= \frac{0.254}{63.5}$$

$$= 4.0 \times 10^{-3}\,\text{mol}$$

This tells us that $8.0 \times 10^{-3}$ moles of electrons will discharge $4.0 \times 10^{-3}$ moles of copper. Therefore 2 moles of electrons are required to discharge 1 mole of copper, and so copper ions have a charge of 2+.

### SAQ 3.4

The same current was passed through aqueous silver nitrate for the same time as in the example above, and 0.863 g of silver was collected. Calculate the charge on the silver ion. [$M_r$ for silver is 108.]

# The mass of a substance discharged during electrolysis

We can also use Faraday's laws to calculate the mass of a substance discharged at an electrode during electrolysis.

As an example of this type of calculation, we shall consider the electrolysis of aqueous silver nitrate. A current of 0.1 A was passed through this solution for 45 minutes. How much silver is deposited at the cathode? [$M_r$ for silver is 108.]

At the cathode:

$$Ag^+(aq) + e^- \longrightarrow Ag(s)$$

The first thing is to calculate the quantity of charge. Using

$$Q = It$$

we substitute $I = 0.1\,\text{A}$ and $t = 45$ minutes $= 2700\,\text{s}$. So

$$Q = 0.1 \times 2700$$

$$= 270\,\text{C}$$

Then,

$$\text{number of moles of electrons} = \frac{Q}{F}$$

$$= \frac{270}{96\,500}$$

$$= 2.80 \times 10^{-3}\,\text{mol}$$

Now look at the cathode equation. One mole of electrons will produce one mole of silver. Therefore, in our example

$$2.80 \times 10^{-3}\,\text{mol of silver are produced}$$

The molar mass of silver is $108\,\text{g}\,\text{mol}^{-1}$. Therefore

$$\text{mass of silver} = 2.80 \times 10^{-3} \times 108$$

$$= 0.30\,\text{g}$$

# The electrolysis of water and sulphuric acid

When water is electrolysed, hydrogen is given off at the cathode and oxygen is given off at the anode:

at the cathode
$$4H_2O(l) + 4e^- \longrightarrow 4OH^-(aq) + 2H_2(g)$$

at the anode
$$2H_2O(l) \longrightarrow 4H^+(aq) + O_2(g) + 4e^-$$

Notice here that the cathode reaction and anode reaction must involve the same number of electrons, so that the whole process is balanced (this is why the cathode reaction has not been divided by 2 throughout).

Sometimes dilute sulphuric acid is added to water before it is electrolysed. This increases the number of $H^+$ ions present, so that hydrogen ions are discharged at the cathode:

at the cathode
$$2H^+(aq) + 2e^- \longrightarrow H_2(g)$$

but oxygen gas is still liberated at the anode. The sulphate ions are not discharged.

## The volume of gas liberated during electrolysis

How do we calculate the volume of oxygen given off during the electrolysis of acidified water, if a current of 0.200 A is passed for 6 hours at room temperature?

The first thing to do is to look at the equation for the reaction at the anode, which tells us that 4 moles of electrons are involved in the liberation of 1 mole of oxygen.

We now work out the charge passed. Using $Q = It$, with $I = 0.2$ A and $t = 6$ hours $= 21\,600$ s:

$$Q = 0.2 \times 21\,600$$
$$= 4.32 \times 10^3 \, C$$

Then using

$$\text{number of moles of electrons} = \frac{Q}{F}$$

$$= \frac{4.32 \times 10^3}{96\,500}$$

$$= 0.0448 \, \text{mol}$$

Now, if 4 moles of electrons give 1 mole of oxygen, $O_2$, then 0.0448 moles of electrons give $\frac{1}{4} \times 0.0448$ moles of oxygen, $O_2$
$$= 0.0112 \text{ moles of oxygen, } O_2$$
One mole of oxygen occupies 24.0 dm³ at room temperature. Therefore
0.0112 moles of oxygen occupy $24.0 \times 0.0112 \, \text{dm}^3$
$$= 0.269 \, \text{dm}^3$$

### SAQ 3.5

A current of 1.40 A was passed through aqueous lead nitrate for 1 hour at room temperature. Calculate the mass of lead collected at the cathode and the volume of oxygen collected at the anode. [$M_r$ for Pb is 207, $F = 96\,500$ C, 1 mole of $O_2$ occupies 24.0 dm³.]

# Determining the Avogadro constant $L$ by electrolysis

The Avogadro constant $L$ is the number of particles in 1 mole. It has a value of $6.022 \times 10^{23} \, \text{mol}^{-1}$. Using electrolysis, it is possible to obtain this value for $L$ both easily and accurately.

The apparatus is shown in *figure 3.5* – it is the electrolysis of copper sulphate solution already discussed earlier in this chapter. The electrodes are both made from copper foil, and it is important that the foil is very clean. Before the electrolysis is started, both electrodes are weighed so that the mass of each is known. A current of 0.2 A is then passed through the solution for 30 minutes – both

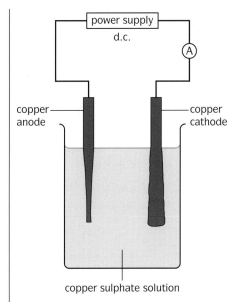

● *Figure 3.5* The electrolysis of aqueous copper sulphate can be used to calculate the value of the Avogadro constant.

the current and the time must be measured precisely because they are used to calculate the charge passed. The electrodes are then weighed again.

Now the charge passed during the electrolysis is calculated as shown above.

The mass of copper deposited at the cathode is calculated by weighing.

At the cathode:
$$Cu^{2+}(aq) + 2e^- \longrightarrow Cu(s)$$

We now know the amount of charge required to deposit a fixed mass of copper.

We can now calculate the amount of charge required to deposit 63.5 g of copper (1 mole of copper). If we divide this amount of charge by the charge on one electron ($1.6 \times 10^{-19}$ C) this tells us how many moles of electrons are used to deposit 63.5 g of copper (1 mole).

Look at the equation for the reaction: 2 moles of electrons are required to deposit 1 mole of copper atoms. Therefore divide the number of moles of electrons calculated above by 2. This gives the Avogadro number *L*.

### SAQ 3.6

In this experiment to calculate *L*:

a What do you predict about the changes in mass of the anode and the cathode in this experiment?

b Why are both the anode and cathode weighed?

c Why is it important that the electrodes are clean?

d What are the units of *L*?

# Electrolysis in industry

## *The chlor–alkali industry*

The chlor–alkali industry produces chlorine, sodium hydroxide and hydrogen by the electrolysis of brine, which is a concentrated solution of rock salt (sodium chloride) in water. This process is often done in an electrolytic cell called a diaphragm cell, although this is slowly being replaced by a more modern membrane cell. All three products are used in huge quantities by the chemical industry.

■ *Some uses of chlorine*
  Water purification
  Bleach – in industry mainly for paper products such as tissues, writing paper and nappies, and for domestic cleaners
  Chemicals such as poly(chloroethene) and tetrachloromethane
■ *Some uses of sodium hydroxide*
  Chemicals such as sodium cyanide and tetraethyl-lead
  Rayon and acetate fibres
  Paper
  Soap and detergents
■ *Some uses of hydrogen*
  Production of ammonia, methanol and nylon
  Refining petroleum
  Fuel

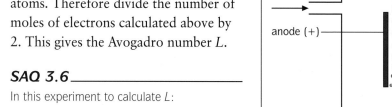

● *Figure 3.6* The diaphragm cell.

## *The diaphragm cell*

In this cell (*figure 3.6*) an asbestos diaphragm separates the anode and cathode. The anode is made from titanium, sometimes with a coating of platinum, and the cathode is made from steel.

In the anode compartment fresh brine, containing $Na^+$ and $Cl^-$ ions, is introduced. Chlorine is given off as the chloride ions are oxidised:

$$2Cl^-(aq) \longrightarrow Cl_2(g) + 2e^-$$

In the cathode compartment hydrogen gas and hydroxide ions are released:

$$2H_2O(l) + 2e^- \longrightarrow 2OH^-(aq) + H_2(g)$$

The spent (used-up) brine moves from the anode to the cathode and sodium hydroxide solution is taken out. However, some chloride ions escape into the cathode compartment through the diaphragm, and so the sodium hydroxide is contaminated with about 15% sodium chloride, which has to be removed later. The hydroxide solution must also be concentrated before it can be used by other chemical industries, so these two factors increase the cost of the process.

The purpose of the diaphragm is to prevent the chlorine and hydroxide ions mixing, because this would lead to the production of bleach – sodium hypochlorite solution, NaOCl (this reaction is discussed in chapter 5). The diaphragm also prevents hydroxide ions from reaching the anode, where they can be discharged to give oxygen gas – which would contaminate the chlorine. The diaphragm is made of asbestos because the cell operates at high temperatures and the solutions are very corrosive. (See *box 1B* on asbestos on page 10.)

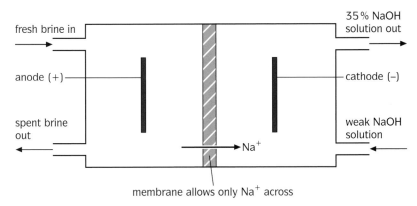

● **Figure 3.7** The membrane cell.

## The membrane cell

The membrane cell *(figure 3.7)* has certain advantages over the diaphragm cell. In this cell brine is electrolysed as in the diaphragm cell, with the same anode and cathode reactions. However, the diaphragm is replaced by a membrane, made of synthetic polymers, which is designed to allow cations to pass through but not anions. Therefore the sodium ions can pass through the membrane, so a current is carried across, but the chloride ions and hydroxide ions cannot pass. This means that the sodium hydroxide solution produced is not contaminated with sodium chloride, and does not have to be purified at a later stage. Like asbestos, the membrane is also resistant to corrosive solutions and the high temperatures that operate inside the cell.

The brine circulates in the anode compartment. In the cathode compartment, weak aqueous sodium hydroxide is introduced and the more concentrated 35% sodium hydroxide solution, produced by the electrolysis, is removed.

## *Purifying aluminium*

Aluminium is usually purified from the ore bauxite, which contains around 50% aluminium oxide, $Al_2O_3$. The first stage in the process is

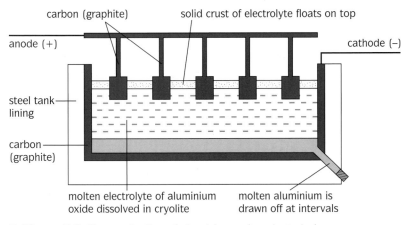

● **Figure 3.8** The production of aluminium using electrolysis.

to separate the aluminium oxide from the other constituents of the ore. Next, the $Al^{3+}$ ions in aluminium oxide have to be reduced to aluminium, but electrolysis cannot be used to do this directly because the melting point of aluminium oxide is over 2000 °C, which is too high to make the process economic. Instead, the aluminium oxide is dissolved in molten cryolite (another aluminium-containing ore), which reduces the temperature of the electrolytic process to 850–950°C.

The cathode is made of graphite-lined steel *(figure 3.8)*, and here the aluminium ions are reduced:

$$Al^{3+}(l) + 3e^- \longrightarrow Al(l)$$

The purified aluminium is molten and can be drawn off periodically from the bottom of the electrolysis cell.

The anode is made of graphite, and here oxygen is produced:

$$2O^{2-}(l) \longrightarrow O_2(g) + 4e^-$$

The oxygen attacks the graphite anode and forms carbon dioxide, so the electrodes are renewed every other day.

This entire process is expensive because electricity is used to drive the electrolysis and also to keep the aluminium oxide/cryolite mixture molten. Very high currents of around 100 000 A are used. However, aluminium can be readily recycled, which at least reduces the amount of energy and cost involved in separating the aluminium oxide from bauxite. (See the section on recycling of aluminium in chapter 1.)

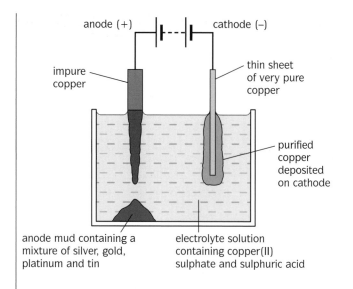

● *Figure 3.9* The refining of copper using electrolysis.

## *Purifying copper*

After copper-containing ores have been mined they are treated to remove impurities such as iron and sulphur, and the copper compounds are reduced to copper, known as 'blister copper'. Although blister copper is 99% pure, the impurities reduce its electrical conductivity so it cannot be used to make electrical cables – its main use – and it is also not pure enough for the manufacture of alloys. The remaining impurities are precious metals such as silver, gold and platinum, and other metals such as iron and nickel. They are removed by electrolysis.

The impure copper is made the anode of an electrolytic cell *(figure 3.9)*, and the cathode is a very thin sheet of *pure* copper. The electrolyte is an aqueous solution of sulphuric acid ($2\,mol\,dm^{-3}$) and copper(II) sulphate ($0.3\,mol\,dm^{-3}$).

At the anode, impure copper is oxidised to $Cu^{2+}$:

$$Cu(s) \longrightarrow Cu^{2+}(aq) + 2e^-$$
impure<br>copper

At the cathode, the $Cu^{2+}$ ions are reduced back to copper:

$$Cu^{2+}(aq) + 2e^- \longrightarrow Cu(s)$$
pure<br>copper

Therefore the impure copper anode gradually disappears as the pure copper is deposited on the thin copper cathode. The copper deposited on the cathode is at least 99.99% pure.

In this process some impurities fall to the bottom of the cell underneath the anode as a sludge, called anode mud. The sludge contains silver, gold, platinum and tin – which means that a profitable by-product of copper refining is the reclaiming of precious metals from the anode mud. Other impurities like iron and nickel are soluble, so the electrolyte has to be continually purified to prevent them from being deposited on the cathode.

## SUMMARY

- Electrolysis means a chemical change in a liquid or solution caused by an electric current.

- When molten sodium chloride is electrolysed, sodium is discharged at the cathode and chlorine is discharged at the anode.

- When aqueous solutions are electrolysed, the ions that are discharged depend on the concentration of the solution and the reducing power of the ion.

- Water can be electrolysed: hydrogen is discharged at the cathode and oxygen is discharged at the anode.

- Electroplating is a process in which the object to be plated is made the cathode in an electrolytic cell containing a solution of the plating metal, so that the plating metal is deposited on the cathode.

- The Faraday constant $F$ is the charge carried by one mole of electrons: $F = Le$.

- The Avogadro constant $L$ can be determined by electrolysis.

- The quantity of charge, and the mass or volume of substance liberated at each electrode during electrolysis, can be calculated.

- Electrolysis is used in the chemical industry to produce chlorine and sodium hydroxide from brine, and to purify aluminium and copper from their ores.

## Questions

1 During the electrolysis of a $1\,mol\,dm^{-3}$ solution of copper(II) sulphate, a current of $0.100\,A$ was passed for 1 hour.
  a Calculate the amount of copper deposited at the cathode.
  b What is the substance discharged at the anode? Calculate the amount.

2 What mass of each of the following substances is discharged by the passage of 0.300 moles of electrons?
  a Copper from copper sulphate.
  b Magnesium from magnesium chloride.
  c Hydrogen from aqueous sodium chloride.

3 The same current was passed through molten sodium chloride and molten aluminium oxide for the same amount of time, and $2.30\,g$ of sodium was deposited. What mass of aluminium was deposited?

# The Group II elements and their compounds

1 outline the normal physical properties of the Group II elements magnesium to barium;

2 describe the reactions of these elements with oxygen and water;

3 describe the acid–base reactions of the oxides with water;

4 describe the trend in thermal stability of the carbonates and nitrates;

5 explain this trend in terms of the charge density of the metal ion and the polarisability of the anion;

6 describe the trend in solubilities of the sulphates;

7 explain this trend by comparing the values of the lattice enthalpy and the enthalpy change of hydration;

8 describe some uses of these elements and their compounds in industry and agriculture;

9 interpret trends in the properties of these elements, and make predictions from these trends.

## Introduction

The elements of Group II are often called the **alkaline earth metals**. They are:

| | | |
|---|---|---|
| beryllium | Be | $[He]2s^2$ |
| magnesium | Mg | $[Ne]3s^2$ |
| calcium | Ca | $[Ar]4s^2$ |
| strontium | Sr | $[Kr]5s^2$ |
| barium | Ba | $[Xe]6s^2$ |
| radium | Ra | $[Rn]7s^2$ |

Beryllium is markedly different from the other members of the Group, and so we shall not consider it here. We also shall not consider radium (the element discovered and isolated by Marie Curie), as all its isotopes are radioactive.

The alkaline earth metals from magnesium to barium are white metals, with low melting and boiling points compared to transition metals like iron. They are good conductors of heat and electricity. The white colour is an oxide film – the metals themselves are shiny but react quickly with air, and the oxide film prevents the metals from reacting further. These metals burn in air with characteristic flame colours – magnesium white, calcium brick-red, strontium red and barium green. Their physical properties are listed in *table 4.1*.

The metals of Group II all have two electrons in their outer s subshell, and these are lost when the metal reacts. This means that they always form an ion of oxidation number +2 in their compounds, such as $Mg^{2+}$ and $Ca^{2+}$. It also means that they are less reactive than Group I metals, because they have to lose two valence electrons, whereas Group I metals lose only one. The outer s electrons are also the reason for the relatively low melting and boiling points – the atomic radii are large because the outer electrons are held weakly by the nucleus, and this increased atomic size means that the attractive forces between atoms in the metal lattice are weak.

### SAQ 4.1

Predict and explain the trend in electronegativity of the Group II elements.

| Element | Mg | Ca | Sr | Ba |
|---|---|---|---|---|
| Atomic number | 12 | 20 | 38 | 56 |
| Metallic radius/nm | 0.160 | 0.197 | 0.215 | 0.224 |
| Ionic radius/nm | 0.072 | 0.100 | 0.113 | 0.136 |
| First ionisation energy/kJ mol$^{-1}$ | 738 | 590 | 550 | 503 |
| Second ionisation energy/kJ mol$^{-1}$ | 1451 | 1145 | 1064 | 965 |
| Third ionisation energy/kJ mol$^{-1}$ | 7733 | 4912 | 4210 | |
| Melting point/°C | 649 | 839 | 769 | 725 |
| Boiling point/°C | 1107 | 1484 | 1384 | 1640 |

● **Table 4.1** Physical properties of Group II elements

## SAQ 4.2

Sketch and explain a bar chart showing the first three ionisation energies of calcium.

The standard electrode potentials of the alkaline earth elements ($E^{\ominus}_{M^{2+}/M}$) range from $-2.37\,\text{V}$ to $-2.90\,\text{V}$ *(table 4.2)*. This shows that they are strongly reducing metals, and this property dominates their chemistry.

### Box 4A Marie Curie

Marie Curie, *née* Marja Skłodowska, was born in Poland in 1867. Her first job was as a governess, which she took to pay for her sister's medical training in France. After her sister qualified Marie also went to Paris to study at the Sorbonne, where she obtained the highest marks in physics. She also met and married Pierre Curie, who was a research scientist.

Marie Curie suspected that in the uranium ore called pitchblende there was another radioactive substance as well as uranium. She treated tonnes of pitchblende and eventually isolated a small quantity of radium chloride – radium was unknown before this. Pierre Curie helped her in this work, which was remarkable in its detective work, as 10 tonnes of pitchblende contain about 1 g of radium. The Curies were awarded the Nobel Prize in 1903 (along with Becquerel, who discovered radio-activity in 1896) for this work.

In 1906 Pierre, by then Professor of Physics at the Sorbonne, was killed by a horse-drawn carriage and Marie took over his post. She was the first woman to hold this position. In 1911 she was awarded a second Nobel Prize for her discovery of radium and polonium (which she named after Poland). The Curies' daughter Irene, with her husband Frederic Joliot, was also awarded a Nobel Prize for chemistry in 1935.

● *Figure 4.1* Marie Curie.

| Element | $E^{\ominus}_{M^{2+}/M}$/V | |
|---|---|---|
| magnesium | −2.37 | Increasing reducing |
| calcium | −2.87 | properties down |
| strontium | −2.89 | the Group |
| barium | −2.90 | |

● *Table 4.2* Standard electrode potentials of Group II elements in contact with solutions of their ions

These values confirm that, in all their reactions, the Group II metals will be oxidised to their ions:

$$M(s) \longrightarrow M^{2+} + 2e^-$$

The oxidation number of the oxidised state is always +2, and in compounds the metals are always found as the $M^{2+}$ ion.

## Summary of general properties

The general properties of the Group II elements magnesium to barium are as follows:

- They are all metals.
- They are good conductors of heat and electricity.
- Their compounds are all white or colourless.
- In all their compounds they have an oxidation number +2.
- Their compounds are ionic.
- Their oxides and hydroxides are basic.
- They react with acids to give hydrogen.

Compared with the metals of Group I:

- They are harder and denser.
- They have higher melting points.
- They exhibit stronger metallic bonding (because they have two valence electrons instead of one).

## Uses

The elements of Group II and their compounds are widely used in many varied ways in commerce and industry.

*Magnesium* burns with a bright white light, and is used in flares, incendiary bombs and tracer bullets. It was once used in photographic flash bulbs.

*Magnesium* has such a strong reducing power that it is widely used as a sacrificial anode on steel objects such as ships, outboard motors and bridges (this is discussed under 'The rusting of iron' in chapter 2). Its strong reducing power also means that it can be used to extract less electropositive metals such as titanium in the Kroll process, which takes place at 1000 °C under an argon atmosphere:

$$2Mg(s) + TiCl_4(g) \longrightarrow Ti(s) + 2MgCl_2(l)$$

*Magnesium* is also found in chlorophyll, the substance in plants which performs photosynthesis.

*Magnesium hydroxide* is a weak alkali and is used in indigestion remedies and in toothpastes, where it helps to neutralise acids in the mouth which encourage tooth decay.

*Magnesium oxide* is a refractory material, which means that it is resistant to heat (its melting point is over 2800 °C). Its main use is for the lining of furnaces.

*Magnesium fluoride* is used to coat the surface of camera lenses, to reduce the amount of reflected light. It is responsible for the violet colour on the surface of the lens.

*Calcium carbonate* is an important compound as it is used in making cement – see *box 4B*, page 45.

*Lime* or *quicklime*, which is *calcium oxide*, is also used in cement, mortar *(figure 4.2)* and plaster manufacture, but its main use is in agriculture. It is spread on the soil in vast quantities to reduce the acidity of the soil. This increases crop yields. It is the origin of the theatrical term 'limelight', because it glows with a bright white light when strongly heated and was originally used in stage lighting.

*Calcium carbide* is used to prepare acetylene (ethyne), which is one of the most important chemicals used in organic synthesis.

*Lime water*, a solution of *calcium hydroxide*, is used as a laboratory test for carbon dioxide gas.

*Solid calcium hydroxide* is also used on acidic soil, and in the construction industry as a component of lime mortar, which is a mixture of sand and calcium hydroxide in water.

*Calcium oxide* has a very important role in purifying iron, as it reacts with impurities in the ore to form a molten slag:

$$CaO(s) + SiO_2(s) \longrightarrow CaSiO_3(l)$$

basic    acidic
oxide    oxide

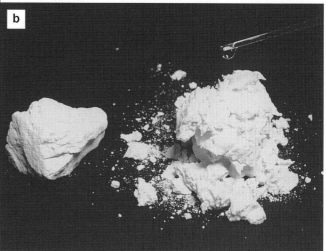

● *Figure 4.2*
**a** Calcium oxide is used in mortar.
**b** Addition of water to dry calcium oxide causes the solid to crumble, in an exothermic reaction producing calcium hydroxide.

*Plaster of Paris*, used to set broken bones and for modelling, is an insoluble form of *calcium sulphate*, $2CaSO_4.H_2O$. When it is mixed with water, it hydrates to $CaSO_4.2H_2O$ and sets hard.

The *hydrogencarbonates of calcium and magnesium* are responsible for the hardness of water – the metal ions are originally picked up when rain-water trickles over limestone and other similar rocks.

*Barium sulphate* is insoluble and, in suspension, is given to patients as a 'barium meal'. The barium ions coat the walls of the stomach and digestive tract and, as they are opaque to X-rays, they make any imperfections visible by X-ray photography. Soluble barium compounds are toxic, but barium sulphate is safe to use because its solubility is so low – for this reason, it is also used as a laboratory test for the sulphate ion.

*Strontium* has few uses. However, the isotope $^{90}_{38}$Sr has been well studied, as it is produced in many nuclear reactions.

---

### Names of calcium compounds

Several calcium compounds have common names based on the word 'lime', derived from limestone, which is one of the most widespread types of rock:

| | | |
|---|---|---|
| limestone | calcium carbonate | $CaCO_3$ |
| quicklime | calcium oxide | $CaO$ |
| slaked lime | solid calcium hydroxide | $Ca(OH)_2(s)$ |
| lime water | a solution of calcium hydroxide (only sparingly soluble) | $Ca(OH)_2(aq)$ |

---

# The reactions of the Group II metals with water

All these metals reduce water to hydrogen. The reaction with magnesium occurs readily with steam:

$$Mg(s) + H_2O(g) \longrightarrow MgO(s) + H_2(g)$$

The other metals react readily with water and form a cloudy white suspension of the hydroxide (which is sparingly soluble):

$$Ca(s) + 2H_2O(l) \longrightarrow Ca(OH)_2(s) + H_2(g)$$

The reaction with dilute acids is similar – all the metals displace hydrogen from dilute acids as we would expect, as they are all above hydrogen in the reactivity series. For example

$$\underset{\text{magnesium}}{Mg(s)} + \underset{\substack{\text{sulphuric} \\ \text{acid}}}{H_2SO_4(aq)} \longrightarrow \underset{\substack{\text{magnesium} \\ \text{sulphate}}}{MgSO_4(aq)} + \underset{\text{hydrogen}}{H_2(g)}$$

### SAQ 4.3

Write the ionic equation for the reaction of magnesium with dilute acid (given above). Indicate any change in oxidation numbers.

# The reactions of the Group II metals with oxygen

The reactions of these metals with oxygen, once started, are vigorous. The oxide is formed. For example

$$\underset{\text{magnesium}}{2Mg(s)} + \underset{\text{oxygen}}{O_2(g)} \longrightarrow \underset{\substack{\text{magnesium} \\ \text{oxide}}}{2MgO(s)}$$

The Group II metal oxides are all white solids, and they are normally prepared by heating the carbonates or hydroxides. The high charge on the metal cation results in a high lattice enthalpy and a high melting point.

### SAQ 4.4

Some magnesium ribbon (0.2 g) was heated in a crucible until it began to burn. When the burning finished, a white powder remained in the crucible. What is this white powder? Calculate the mass of powder you would expect to find.

# The reactions of the oxides with water

The general reaction of the metal oxides with water is

$$MO(s) + H_2O(l) \longrightarrow M(OH)_2(aq)$$

so that the hydroxide is formed.

Both magnesium oxide and magnesium hydroxide are only sparingly soluble in water – they both have a solubility of only $0.2 \times 10^{-4}$ mol per 100 g of water. Magnesium hydroxide forms a milky-white suspension in water called milk of magnesia and is useful because, as a mild alkali, it is used to alleviate acid indigestion.

When water is added to calcium oxide the oxide swells and steams, and eventually disintegrates into a white powder, which is calcium hydroxide (slaked lime):

$$CaO(s) + H_2O(l) \longrightarrow Ca(OH)_2(s)$$

Slaked lime is used in agriculture to increase the pH of acidic soils and thereby optimise growing conditions and crop yields.

| Element | Solubility of the hydroxide (mole per 100g of water) |
|---|---|
| magnesium | $0.2 \times 10^{-4}$ |
| calcium | $15.3 \times 10^{-4}$ |
| strontium | $33.7 \times 10^{-4}$ |
| barium | $150.0 \times 10^{-4}$ |

● **Table 4.3** The solubilities of the hydroxides of Group II elements

Calcium hydroxide dissolved in water is called lime water and is used to test for the acidic gas carbon dioxide, which produces calcium carbonate:

$$Ca(OH)_2(aq) + CO_2(g) \longrightarrow CaCO_3(s) + H_2O(l)$$

Calcium carbonate is seen as a white suspension.

The hydroxides are increasingly soluble as the Group is descended *(table 4.3)*, and so the pH of the aqueous hydroxides increases too.

# The stability of the carbonates and nitrates to heat

The Group II metals form metal carbonates of formula $MCO_3$ and metal nitrates of formula $M(NO_3)_2$.

When heated, the carbonates decompose to form the metal oxide and carbon dioxide gas:

$$MCO_3(s) \longrightarrow MO(s) + CO_2(g)$$

When heated, the nitrates decompose to form the metal oxide, nitrogen dioxide gas and oxygen gas:

$$2M(NO_3)_2(s) \longrightarrow 2MO(s) + 4NO_2(g) + O_2(g)$$

Both the carbonates and the nitrates decompose at higher temperatures as the Group is descended.

How do we explain this trend? We do so by relating it to the size of the metal ion and its **polarising power**. Small ions have greater polarising power than large ions, because the **charge density** of a small ion is greater. Both the carbonate and the nitrate anions are large, with diffuse electron clouds, and this makes them **easily polarisable**. So the small magnesium ion can polarise the large anion, attracting the electrons

towards it – this distorts the shape of the anion, which encourages decomposition. The large barium ion, however, has little tendency to polarise the anion, and decomposition is not as favoured. The other metal ions fall between these two extremes, and so the decomposition temperatures rise as the Group is descended.

Another factor to be taken into account is the **stability of the metal oxide** – remember that both the carbonates and the nitrates decompose to give the oxide. The largest lattice energy for a metal oxide is at the top of the Group, because both magnesium ions and oxide ions are small and highly charged. So in addition to magnesium carbonate (or nitrate) having a distorted anion, the product of the decomposition is energetically favoured – again, the decomposition is favoured.

*Figure 4.3* summarises these two factors.

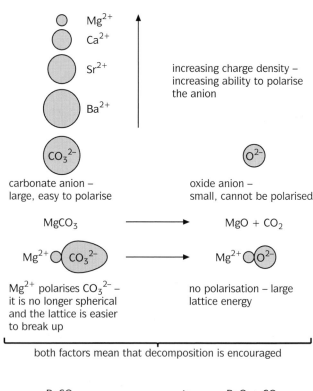

● **Figure 4.3** The factors influencing the decomposition of the carbonates of Group II elements.

## SAQ 4.5

Predict the trend in stability of the hydroxides of the Group II metals when they are heated.

---

### Box 4B Cement

Calcium carbonate occurs in vast quantities in sedimentary rocks, such as limestone, chalk and dolomite. Marble is also a form of calcium carbonate, in which the marbling effect is caused by the presence of iron oxides. However, the largest use of calcium carbonate is the manufacture of cement.

Cement is made by heating a finely ground mixture of limestone with clay (aluminosilicate) at 1500°C in a rotary kiln. This process results in clinker, which is reground and mixed with about 3% gypsum (calcium sulphate). This is a complex process, and the final formula of cement can be regarded as

$$2Ca_3SiO_5 + Ca_3Al_2O_6$$

The setting of cement is also a complex process – the cement reacts with water and carbon dioxide from the air.

The annual production of cement worldwide is about 1 billion tonnes.

---

# The solubilities of the sulphates

The Group II metals form sulphates with the general formula $MSO_4$.

The sulphates of the Group II metals become less soluble as the Group is descended. This is shown in *table 4.4*. Notice that this is the opposite trend to the solubility of the hydroxides.

This trend can be explained by considering two enthalpy changes – the **lattice energy** and the **enthalpy change of hydration**. They are the main energy changes involved when an ionic solid is put into water and the ions are pulled apart by water molecules (a process called **solvation**).

| Element | Solubility of the sulphate (mole per 100g of water) |
|---|---|
| magnesium | $1830 \times 10^{-4}$ |
| calcium | $11 \times 10^{-4}$ |
| strontium | $0.71 \times 10^{-4}$ |
| barium | $0.009 \times 10^{-4}$ |

● **Table 4.4** The solubilities of the sulphates of Group II elements

The first stage in this process is to separate the ions:

$$M^{2+}SO_4^{2-}(s) \longrightarrow M^{2+}(g) + SO_4^{2-}(g)$$

which is the **reverse of lattice formation**. This is an **endothermic reaction** – it requires energy. As the ionic radius increases, the enthalpy change of this lattice separation becomes less endothermic.

The second stage is the **hydration** of the separate ions, when they are surrounded by water molecules. This is an **exothermic reaction** – it releases energy. As the charge density of the cation decreases on descending the Group, this enthalpy change becomes less exothermic. Small, highly charged ions have large enthalpy changes of hydration because such ions can attract larger numbers of water molecules. So at the top of the Group the endothermic enthalpy change of lattice separation is large, but the exothermic enthalpy change of hydration more than compensates for this and the sulphate has a high solubility. At the bottom of the Group, although the endothermic enthalpy change of lattice separation is lower, the enthalpy change of hydration is not exothermic enough to give such a high solubility.

*Figure 4.4* shows these energy changes.

## SAQ 4.6

Predict the trend in the solubilities of the nitrates of the Group II elements.

---

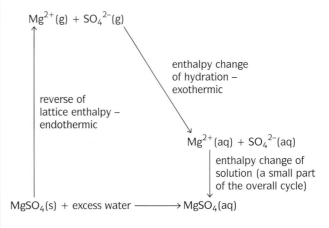

● **Figure 4.4** The energy changes involved in dissolving a salt, magnesium sulphate.

# SUMMARY

- The Group II elements magnesium to barium are called the alkaline earth elements.

- They have standard metallic properties such as conduction of heat and electricity, high melting point and liberation of hydrogen from acids.

- They are strongly reducing metals, as shown by their standard electrode potentials. In all reactions they form the $M^{2+}$ ion only.

- They react with water and acids to give hydrogen gas and the metal hydroxide.

- Several compounds of the Group II elements are commercially important, for example calcium carbonate is used in manufacturing cement, calcium hydroxide is used in agriculture and magnesium oxide is used to line furnaces.

- The decomposition temperature of the carbonates and nitrates increases as the Group is descended – this trend is explained by considering the polarising effect of the metal ion on the anions involved.

- The sulphates become less soluble as the Group is descended – this trend is explained by considering the values of the lattice enthalpies and the enthalpy change of hydration.

# Questions

1 On the basis of your knowledge of Group II, predict in Group I:
   a the element that reacts most vigorously with water;
   b the solubility of the compounds with water;
   c the element with the least stable carbonate when heated.

2 The element radium, Ra, is a Group II element. Predict:
   a its appearance;
   b its reaction with water;
   c its reaction with oxygen;
   d the reaction of its oxide with water;
   e the thermal stability of its carbonate.

3 a Write equations to show how, beginning with limestone, quicklime and slaked lime are formed.
   b Explain how slaked lime is used to make lime water, and write the equation showing how lime water reacts with carbon dioxide gas to give a milky precipitate.
   c This milky precipitate eventually disappears if carbon dioxide is bubbled through lime water for a long time. What reaction do you think is occurring between the precipitate and the carbon dioxide?

# The Group IV elements and their compounds

## Introduction

The elements of Group IV are:

| | | |
|---|---|---|
| carbon | C | $[He]2s^22p^2$ |
| silicon | Si | $[Ne]3s^23p^2$ |
| germanium | Ge | $[Ar]3d^{10}4s^24p^2$ |
| tin | Sn | $[Kr]4d^{10}5s^25p^2$ |
| lead | Pb | $[Xe]4f^{14}5d^{10}6s^26p^2$ |

Group IV is possibly the most interesting Group in the Periodic Table in the way that trends and patterns between the elements occur. Broadly speaking, in the other Groups the elements all have similar properties, and certain trends in these properties are apparent. But in Group IV the elements are very different from one another. The most striking difference is the change from non-metallic carbon at the top of the Group, to metallic tin and lead at the bottom. In between, silicon and germanium are known as metalloids because their properties fall between those of non-metals and those of metals.

This trend shows itself in three main ways:

■ Carbon has an extended covalent structure (in diamond and graphite) whereas lead has a typically metallic close-packed structure.

■ The oxides of carbon ($CO_2$) and silicon ($SiO_2$) are acidic, which is a typical feature of non-metals, whereas the oxides of tin ($SnO_2$) and lead ($PbO_2$) are amphoteric (they can behave both as acids and as bases).

■ The compounds of carbon and silicon are covalent, typical of non-metals, whereas tin and lead form ionic compounds containing $Sn^{2+}$ and $Pb^{2+}$ ions, typical of metals.

The physical properties are summarised in *table 5.1*.

| Element | C | Si | Ge | Sn | Pb |
|---|---|---|---|---|---|
| Atomic radius/nm | 0.077 | 0.118 | 0.122 | 0.140 | 0.154 |
| First ionisation energy/kJ mol$^{-1}$ | 1086 | 789 | 762 | 709 | 716 |
| Structure | giant molecular ⟵ | | ⟶ giant metallic ⟶ | | |
| Electrical conductivity | none (diamond) ⟵ fair (graphite) | semiconductor ⟶ | | good | good |
| Melting point/°C | 3652 (graphite) | 1410 | 937 | 232 | 328 |
| Boiling point/°C | 4827 | 2355 | 2830 | 2270 | 1740 |

● **Table 5.1**  Physical properties of Group IV elements

**SAQ 5.1**

Compare the appearances of carbon, tin and lead. Do they reflect the change in character going down Group IV?

# Uses

Carbon and silicon are among the most important of all elements. *Carbon* is very different from the rest of the Group. It is found in all living things because of its ability to **catenate** – carbon atoms join together with strong bonds to form long, complex chain molecules. This is the basis of organic chemistry. *Carbon* in the form of *diamonds* is obviously used in jewellery but is also useful in industry because diamonds are so hard – for example, diamonds form the tips of bits used for oil drilling.

*Graphite*, another form of *carbon*, is used in carbon fibres where it strengthens polymers in lightweight turbine blades, in racing car brakes (*figure 5.1*) and in the hulls of speed boats. *Graphite* is also used as a lubricant at high temperatures and as the 'lead' in pencils. It is often used for inert electrodes, and is used as a 'moderator' for slowing down neutrons in a nuclear reactor.

*Silicon* is the second most abundant element in the Earth's crust (after oxygen) – for instance, sand is silicon dioxide, $SiO_2$.

*Silicon* is used as a semiconductor in the electronics industry, in the form of 'silicon chips'.

● *Figure 5.1* Carbon fibre is used in the brakes of Formula 1 cars. You can see the carbon fibre glow through the wheels as it heats up under heavy braking.

Without this element we would not have the vast amount of computer technology available to us, and our lives would be very different in almost every area (see *box 5A*, page 50).

*Silicon* is also a major component of glass and lubricants.

*Silicones* are silicon-based compounds that are widely used in plastic and cosmetic surgery, although the health risks associated with silicone implants are increasingly being discussed.

*Silicates*, discussed in chapter 1, are used as the basis of ceramics – extremely useful materials in industry for many things including special glasses, parts of engines and temperature-resistant furnaces.

The other elements of Group IV are less important in terms of the amount used in our society. *Germanium*, like silicon, is a semiconductor, but is less widely used. *Tin* and *lead* are metals with several uses. *Tin* is used as a surface layer to protect iron and steel objects, such as in tin cans. It is resistant to acids and so is useful for cans containing soft drinks or fruit, but nowadays aluminium is increasingly being used for cans. *Lead* is a dense, malleable, soft metal, which makes it easy to work. Its main use is for the electrodes in car batteries. It is also used as a screen against radiation in hospital X-ray departments and in industry.

# Oxidation states and bonding

The elements of Group IV have four outer-shell electrons, two electrons in the s subshell and two electrons in the p subshell. They all form compounds in which they have oxidation number +4, such as $CCl_4$ (tetrachloromethane) and $SiO_2$ (silica). In these compounds all four of the outer-shell electrons take part in the bonding.

Tin and lead also occur in compounds with oxidation number +2, such as $SnCl_2$ (tin(II) chloride) and $PbSO_4$ (lead(II) sulphate). This shows us that the **lower oxidation state** becomes **more stable** as the Group is descended. The reason for this is that there is an increasing tendency for the two s electrons not to take part in the bonding, as the atomic size increases. This is called the **inert-pair effect**. The two p electrons are held less tightly as the atomic size and shielding increase, so can be lost to form a +2 ion and give the bonding characteristics of a metal.

Metals are generally good reducing agents, and the reducing powers of tin and lead can be seen from their standard electrode potentials

$$E^{\ominus}_{Sn^{2+}/Sn} = -0.14\,V$$
$$E^{\ominus}_{Pb^{2+}/Pb} = -0.13\,V$$

Both values are negative, which means that both metals can displace hydrogen from acids. This could lead you to believe that lead would be unsuitable as a building material exposed to the rain, which is slightly acidic. However, lead forms an oxide coating, which is insoluble and protects the metal from reacting with rain-water.

## SAQ 5.2

Can lead displace tin from aqueous tin(II) chloride?

Normally the elements of Group IV have a valency of 4 in their compounds, but they can all, except carbon, make more than four bonds. This is because they are able to use a set of d orbitals in their bonding. The d orbitals they use are the empty ones of the outer shell – the 3d set for silicon, the 4d set for germanium and so on. By using these orbitals the element can hold more than

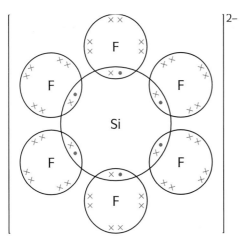

● **Figure 5.2** The bonding in $SiF_6^{2-}$, showing the expansion of the octet of outer-shell electrons. The silicon now has 12 electrons in its outer shell – the extra electrons are accommodated in the 3d levels.

eight electrons in its bonding shell. This is called **expansion of the octet**. It cannot happen in carbon because there are no empty d orbitals available.

The complex ion $SiF_6^{2-}$, shown in *figure 5.2*, illustrates this point. Silicon provides four bonding electrons for four fluorine atoms, and the others are provided by two fluoride ions and occupy the 3d orbitals. These fluoride ions provide two 'extra' electrons, which gives the complex an overall charge of 2−.

## SAQ 5.3

Draw a diagram to show the shape of the $SiF_6^{2-}$ ion.

## SAQ 5.4

The hydrides of the Group IV elements are tetrahedral. Give a simple explanation for this.

# Melting points and electrical conductivities

The **melting points** of the Group IV elements **decrease** on descending the Group. The **electrical conductivity** of these elements **increases** on descending the Group (see *table 5.1*). Both these trends can be explained by considering the type of structure and bonding of each element.

At the top of the Group, carbon has a giant covalent structure. This vast network of strong covalent bonds means that the melting point is very high. It also means that electricity cannot be conducted, as there are no mobile electrons – all the electrons are firmly held in covalent bonds.

At the bottom of the Group, tin and lead have a giant metallic structure. The outer electrons are held less tightly as the distance from the nucleus and shielding are both increased, so they are able to form a delocalised sea of electrons. The melting point is lower because heat energy can be transferred through the lattice fairly easily, and the electrical conductivity is good, as you would expect for a typical metallic structure.

Silicon and germanium are semiconductors – they conduct electricity only under certain circumstances.

## Box 5A  Semiconductors

The first computers were huge structures with wires linking each transistor. Now millions of transistors can be fitted onto a small silicon chip *(figure 5.3)*. This is possible because silicon is a semiconductor.

In metals, the outer-shell electrons occupy orbitals called **conduction bands** that spread throughout the metal. Electrons in the conduction bands are mobile, so when a potential difference is applied to the metal these electrons can move and electricity is carried through the solid. In a material that does not conduct electricity, the electrons are located in **bonding orbitals** and are not mobile. There is a large energy gap, called a **band gap**, between the bonding electrons and the first available empty conduction band in an insulator. In silicon and germanium, the band gap is small enough to make the conduction band accessible, even though it is not normally occupied.

In a semiconductor, a solid that normally does not conduct electricity can be made to conduct by either adding a small supply of extra electrons, or removing a small number of electrons. For instance, germanium is a semiconductor and can be **doped** with gallium or arsenic to make it conduct. These are suitable elements for doping germanium because they are its neighbours in its Period, so they have similar-sized atoms which fit well into the germanium structure. An arsenic atom has one extra electron compared to germanium, and this electron occupies a conduction band. Now, when a potential difference is applied across the solid, it can conduct. This is called an **n-type conductor** (n for negative electrons). A gallium atom has one less electron than germanium, so the solid has fewer electrons overall. We say that gallium introduces positive 'holes', which enable the remaining electrons to move through the solid more easily. This is a **p-type conductor** (p for positive 'holes').

● *Figure 5.3*  This modern silicon chip, the Intel Pentium® Pro, contains 21 million transistors.

## Box 5B  Lead

Lead has been used from ancient times until recently for water pipes – its latin name *'plumbum'* gave water supply workers their name 'plumber'. However, it is now recognised that lead is a cumulative poison, which collects in the brain and impairs its function, and so it is no longer used for water pipes. There is concern that too much lead is present in the atmosphere of cities, released by car exhausts, and that the performance of children at school is affected. For this reason lead-free petrol is now used in most new cars, and many people have converted their cars to run on lead-free fuel. There is a theory that the Roman Empire fell into decline because the Romans were poisoned by lead from their water pipes and no longer had full possession of their senses!

# The tetrachlorides of the Group IV elements

These compounds have the formula $ECl_4$ (E being the Group IV element). They have a simple molecular structure, and the molecules are tetrahedral in shape *(figure 5.4)*. All the tetrachlorides are volatile liquids at room temperature – carbon tetrachloride, also called tetrachloromethane, has a pungent smell and is used as a dry-cleaning fluid. These compounds have low melting and boiling points because the molecules are non-polar so there are no electrostatic forces holding them together.

The **thermal stability** of the tetrachlorides **decreases** on descending the Group as the E–Cl bond gets longer and weaker. We see again that, on

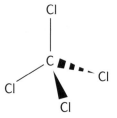

● *Figure 5.4*  The tetrahedral shape of carbon(IV) chloride (carbon tetrachloride). This is the shape expected for a molecule with four covalent bonds and no lone-pairs of electrons, based around a single central atom.

going down the Group, compounds with oxidation number +2 become more stable:

CCl$_4$, SiCl$_4$ and GeCl$_4$ are stable at high temperatures

$$SnCl_4(l) \longrightarrow SnCl_2(s) + Cl_2(g) \quad \text{on heating}$$

$$PbCl_4(l) \longrightarrow PbCl_2(s) + Cl_2(g) \quad \text{near room temperature}$$

## Reaction of the tetrachlorides with water

All the tetrachlorides except CCl$_4$ are **readily hydrolysed** – for example, silicon tetrachloride is immediately converted to silica.

$$SiCl_4(l) + 2H_2O(l) \longrightarrow SiO_2(s) + 4HCl(aq)$$

In these reactions, HCl is always formed.

However, **carbon tetrachloride is completely unaffected by water**. The reason for this difference between CCl$_4$ and the rest of the tetrachlorides is due to electronic structure. When a water molecule attacks silicon tetrachloride (*figure 5.5*), its lone-

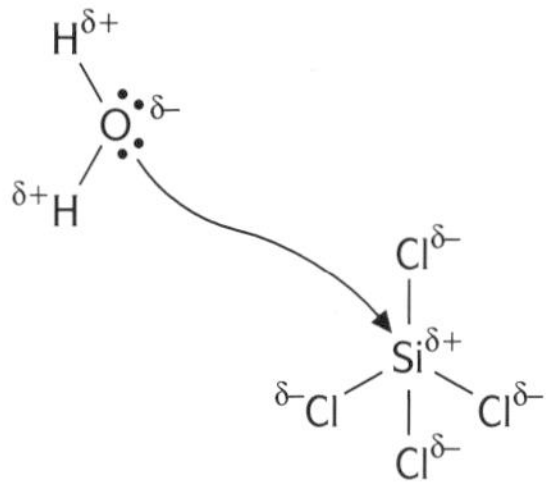

● *Figure 5.5* The reaction of water with silicon(IV) chloride (silicon tetrachloride). A lone-pair of electrons on the oxygen atom in a water molecule attacks the silicon, which has a partial positive charge due to the electron-withdrawing effects of the chlorine atoms. The silicon therefore temporarily has five bonds as part of the reaction mechanism.

pair is attracted to the silicon atom, which has a partial positive charge – the chlorine atoms withdraw electron density. For a short while, the silicon atom has five bonds round it. The extra bond can be placed in the 3d orbital because silicon can expand its octet in this way. However, carbon cannot expand into a d orbital, so a water molecule is unable to bond to carbon in CCl$_4$.

**a** The dioxides – Group IV element has oxidation number of +4

| Oxide | CO$_2$ | SiO$_2$ | GeO$_2$ | SnO$_2$ | PbO$_2$ |
|---|---|---|---|---|---|
| Structure | simple covalent molecules | giant covalent | ← intermediate between giant covalent and ionic → | | |
| Acid–base nature | acidic | acidic | amphoteric | amphoteric | amphoteric |
| Reactions | react with alkalis<br>$CO_2 + 2OH^- \longrightarrow CO_3^{2-} + H_2O$<br>carbonate<br>$SiO_2 + 2OH^- \longrightarrow SiO_3^{2-} + H_2O$<br>silicate | | react with acids and alkalis<br>acids must be concentrated:<br>$SnO_2 + 4H^+ \longrightarrow Sn^{4+} + 2H_2O$<br>alkalis must be molten:<br>$PbO_2 + 2OH^- \longrightarrow PbO_3^{2-} + H_2O$ | | |

**b** The monoxides – Group IV element has oxidation number of +2

| Oxide | CO | SiO | GeO | SnO | PbO |
|---|---|---|---|---|---|
| Structure | simple covalent molecules | simple covalent molecules | ← ionic lattice → | | |
| Acid–base nature | neutral | neutral | amphoteric | amphoteric | amphoteric |
| Reactions | do not react with acids or alkalis | | react with aqueous acids and alkalis to form salts<br>$SnO + 2H^+ \longrightarrow Sn^{2+} + H_2O$<br>$PbO + OH^- + H_2O \longrightarrow Pb(OH)_3^-$ | | |

● *Table 5.2* Properties of the oxides of Group IV elements

*SAQ 5.5*

*SAQ 5.5*_____

The hydrides of Group IV elements become less stable on descending the group. Explain why.

# The oxides of the Group IV elements

The formulae and characteristics of some of the Group IV oxides are shown in *table 5.2*. These compounds have very different structures from one another, from carbon dioxide gas to the ionic lead oxides.

Carbon dioxide and silicon dioxide are **acidic**. Both react with hot concentrated alkali in solution, or with solid pellets of potassium hydroxide or sodium hydroxide. Silica also reacts with metal carbonates to give carbon dioxide:

$$SiO_2(s) + Na_2CO_3(s) \longrightarrow Na_2SiO_3(s) + CO_2(g)$$
sodium<br>silicate

Sodium silicate solution can be turned into a gel by adding dilute acid – this is silica gel and is used as a drying agent, often in sachets to keep electrical goods dry in the box.

As the Group is descended, the oxides become more basic in character. The oxides of germanium and tin are **amphoteric** rather than basic, and react with both acids and alkalis.

The melting points of the dioxides are shown in *table 5.3*. These reflect the great difference there is in the bonding between gaseous carbon dioxide – made up of simple molecules – and the other oxides – all giant structures.

| Oxide | Melting point/°C |
|---|---|
| $CO_2$ | −56 |
| $SiO_2$ | 1610 |
| $GeO_2$ | 1116 |
| $SnO_2$ | 1630 |
| $PbO_2$ | decomposes at 290 |

● *Table 5.3* The melting points of the dioxides of Group IV elements

*SAQ 5.6*_____

If you wanted to make a solution of lead(II) oxide, which acid would you choose?

*SAQ 5.7*_____

Lead(IV) oxide reacts with sulphur dioxide in the following way:

$$PbO_2(s) + SO_2(g) \longrightarrow PbSO_4(s)$$

Is this a redox reaction? If so, identify the species that is oxidised and the species that is reduced.

# SUMMARY

- The Group IV elements differ considerably from one another. The most striking difference is the change in character from non-metals at the top of the Group to metals at the bottom.

- As the Group is descended, the +2 oxidation state becomes more stable than the +4 oxidation state. This is caused by the inert-pair effect.

- All the elements except carbon can expand their octet of outer-shell electrons and form complex ions with more than eight electrons in the outer shell.

- The melting points of the elements decrease and the electrical conductivities increase as the Group is descended. These trends are linked to the structure and bonding of the elements.

- The tetrachlorides are volatile liquids. The molecules have a regular tetrahedral shape.

- All the tetrachlorides except carbon tetrachloride are readily hydrolysed. This mechanism involves expansion of the octet of outer-shell electrons.

- The dioxides go from acidic to amphoteric on descending the Group. The monoxides go from neutral to amphoteric.

- The melting and boiling points of carbon dioxide and carbon monoxide are very low compared with those of the other oxides, reflecting their simple molecular structure.

- Silicon and germanium are semiconductors and have revolutionised computer technology.

# $Q$uestions

1  Use redox potentials to answer the following questions:

   a  Will $Sn^{2+}$ ions reduce $Fe^{3+}$ to $Fe^{2+}$?

   b  Will $Sn^{2+}$ ions reduce $Fe^{2+}$ to Fe?

   c  Will $Cr_2O_7^{2-}$ ions oxidise $Sn^{2+}$ to $Sn^{4+}$?

   Write equations for each redox reaction where appropriate.

2  Tin and chlorine can combine to form the following compounds:

   $SnCl_2$, $SnCl_4$, $SnCl_3^-$, $SnCl_6^{2-}$.

   a  Construct a table to show the oxidation number of tin and the shape of the molecule in each compound.

   b  Write an equation showing a redox reaction for $SnCl_4$.

   c  Write an equation to show the formation of $SnCl_6^{2-}$ from $SnCl_2$.

3  Explain why:

   a  carbon dioxide gas dissolves in water;

   b  silicon dioxide does not dissolve in water;

   c  carbon tetrachloride does not react with water;

   d  silicon tetrachloride reacts vigorously with water.

# The Group VII elements and their compounds

1 describe the appearance of the halogens chlorine, bromine and iodine;

2 explain the trend in their volatility;

3 explain how the standard electrode potentials of the halogens influence their reactivity;

4 describe the reaction of the halogens with sodium thiosulphate, and explain how this reaction with iodine is used as a quantitative test for an oxidising agent;

5 describe how the halogens react with hydrogen to form hydrogen halides;

6 explain how the bond energies of the hydrogen halides affect their thermal stability;

7 describe a test that determines which halide is present;

8 describe the reactions of the aqueous halide ions with concentrated sulphuric acid;

9 describe the reaction of chlorine with cold and hot aqueous sodium hydroxide;

10 explain the change in oxidation number of chlorine in these reactions;

11 explain the importance of the halogens and their compounds in our society.

## Introduction

The elements of Group VII are called the **halogens**:

| | | |
|---|---|---|
| fluorine | F | $[He]2s^2 2p^5$ |
| chlorine | Cl | $[Ne]3s^2 3p^5$ |
| bromine | Br | $[Ar]3d^{10}4s^2 4p^5$ |
| iodine | I | $[Kr]4d^{10}5s^2 5p^5$ |
| astatine | At | $[Xe]4f^{14}5d^{10}6s^2 6p^5$ |

All the isotopes of astatine are radioactive and so this element will not be considered here. Also, we shall not include fluorine in *all* the discussions on Group VII, because its small size and high electronegativity give it some anomalous properties.

The name 'halogen' is derived from the Greek and means 'salt producing'. It was first used at the beginning of the nineteenth century because chlorine, bromine and iodine are all found in the sea as salts. Nowadays we still use the term, because the halogens are very reactive and readily react with metals to form salts.

The halogens are a family of non-metallic elements with some very similar chemical properties, although there are also clear differences between each element. Their reactivity decreases going down the Group. Their chemical characteristics are caused by the outermost seven electrons – two electrons in the s subshell and five electrons in the p subshell. Therefore only one more electron is needed to complete the outer shell of electrons. As a result the most common oxidation state for the halogens is $-1$, although other oxidation states do exist, especially for chlorine, which exhibits a range of oxidation numbers from $-1$ to $+7$. In compounds a halogen atom increases its share of electrons from seven to eight (a full outer shell) by either (a) gaining an electron to form a halide ($Cl^-$, $Br^-$, $I^-$) in ionic compounds, or (b) sharing an electron from another atom in a covalent compound.

The halogen elements form **covalent diatomic molecules**. The atoms are joined by a single covalent bond (*figure 6.1*).

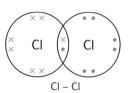

Cl – Cl

● *Figure 6.1* A dot-and-cross diagram of the covalent bonding in chlorine gas.

Fluorine, chlorine and bromine are poisonous. Their melting and boiling points increase with increasing atomic number: fluorine and chlorine are gases at room temperature; bromine is a liquid; and iodine is a solid. This decrease in volatility is the result of increasingly strong van der Waals forces as the relative molecular mass increases.

The colour of the elements deepens with increasing atomic number: fluorine is a pale yellow gas; chlorine is a greenish yellow gas; bromine is a dark red liquid giving off a dense red vapour; iodine is a shiny, grey-black crystalline solid which sublimes to a purple vapour.

The standard electrode potentials of the halogens ($E^{\ominus}_{X_2/2X^-}$) range from $+2.87\,V$ for fluorine to $+0.54\,V$ for iodine. This shows that they are all oxidising agents, and fluorine is the strongest. The oxidising ability is reflected by the reactivity – fluorine is the most reactive halogen. It is also reflected by the electronegativities – fluorine is the most electronegative element, chlorine the third. Look at *table 6.1* for a summary of the physical properties.

## SAQ 6.1

What is the oxidation number of chlorine in $Cl_2$, $CaCl_2$, $Cl_2O_7$ and $ClO_2$?

# Summary of general properties

The general properties of the Group VII elements chlorine, bromine and iodine are as follows:

■ They behave chemically in a similar way.
■ They are non-metals.

■ They all exist as diatomic molecules at room temperature.
■ Their melting and boiling points increase with increasing atomic number.
■ The colour of the elements deepens with increasing atomic number.
■ They are very reactive and readily form salts.
■ In compounds a halogen atom increases its share of electrons from seven to eight by ionic or covalent bonding.
■ The reactivity of the elements decreases on descending the Group.
■ They exhibit a range of oxidation numbers.
■ The electronegativity of the elements decreases on descending the Group.
■ Their oxidising ability decreases on descending the Group.

## SAQ 6.2

Draw dot-and-cross diagrams of NaCl, showing the ionic bond; and of HCl, showing the covalent bond.

# Uses

The commercial and industrial uses of the halogens and their compounds are now outlined.

*Chlorine* is used in vast quantities for many different processes – twenty-nine million tonnes of chlorine are used worldwide annually. Its main uses are in water purification, as a bleach and in the manufacture of various chemicals, as listed in the section on 'Electrolysis in industry' in chapter 3.

One of the classes of organic chemicals made using chlorine is that of CFCs (*chlorofluorocarbons*). CFCs are used as aerosol propellants, refrigerants and as foaming agents in polymers. They are currently being withdrawn from many applications because they are pollutants and are believed to contribute to the destruction of the ozone layer. However, they are useful in at least two ways – they are used in fire extinguishers

| Element | F | Cl | Br | I |
|---|---|---|---|---|
| Atomic radius/nm | 0.071 | 0.099 | 0.114 | 0.133 |
| Ionic radius/nm | 0.133 | 0.180 | 0.195 | 0.215 |
| Electronegativity | 4.0 | 3.0 | 2.8 | 2.5 |
| Electron affinity/kJ mol$^{-1}$ | −328 | −349 | −325 | −295 |
| Melting point/°C | −220 | −101 | −7 | 114 |
| Boiling point/°C | −188 | −35 | 59 | 184 |

● **Table 6.1** Physical properties of Group VII elements. (The electron affinity is the enthalpy change for the process
$X(g) + e^- \longrightarrow X^-(g)$
where X is the halogen)

because they are inert and non-flammable, and they are vital constituents of artificial blood.

Solvents containing chlorine, such as *tetrachloromethane*, $CCl_4$, are widely used to dissolve fats and oils.

*Chlorine* is a good germicide, and is used to kill bacteria in drinking water and swimming pools. Chlorine and some of its compounds are used as domestic and commercial bleaches. In the First World War chlorine and mustard gas ($ClCH_2CH_2SCH_2CH_2Cl$) were used with devastating effect as poison gases. Chlorine is produced by the electrolysis of brine, discussed in chapter 3.

*Fluorine* is used, like chlorine, in CFCs. It is also used to make PTFE (polytetrafluoroethene), which is used as a lubricant and a coating for non-stick cooking pans, electrical insulation and in waterproof clothing.

*Fluoride* ions help to prevent tooth decay. Some children are given fluoride tablets; many toothpastes contain tin fluoride ($SnF_2$); and some water supplies are fluoridated with sodium fluoride.

## The fluoride controversy

Automatic fluoridation of the water we drink has caused some controversy. Many people feel that it is a good thing, as it is one of the factors linked to a reduction in the number of fillings in children's teeth. However, too much fluoride discolours teeth permanently, and can cause liver damage. So some people feel that water supplies should not be fluoridated, but that the freedom to choose to take fluoride supplements or not should be left to the individual *(figure 6.2)*.

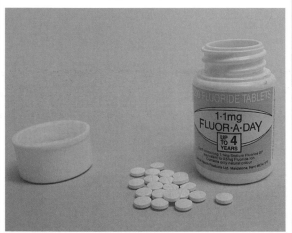

● *Figure 6.2* Flouride tablets are available to add to drinking water, to improve dental health.

*Hydrofluoric acid* (HF) is used to etch glass.

*Bromine* is used in 1,2-dibromoethane ($BrCH_2CH_2Br$), which is a petrol additive.

*Bromochloromethane* ($CH_2ClBr$) is used in fire extinguishers.

*Silver bromide* is used in photographic film.

*Iodine* is an essential part of our diet, and an imbalance can cause thyroid problems.

A solution of *iodine in alcohol* is sometimes used as an antiseptic.

# The reactivity of the halogens: displacement reactions

The decreasing reactivity of the halogens chlorine, bromine and iodine is shown by their decreasing standard electrode potentials *(table 6.2)*. The $E^{\ominus}$ values are for the process

$$X_2(aq) + 2e^- \rightleftharpoons 2X^-(aq)$$

In most of their oxidising reactions the halogens react as $X_2$ molecules and form hydrated halide ions, $X^-(aq)$. As the oxidising ability decreases from chlorine to iodine, any halogen can displace another with a less positive standard electrode potential. This means that, if each halogen is reacted with a halide ion in aqueous solution, a series of displacement reactions occurs.

■ Chlorine displaces bromine and iodine:

$$Cl_2(aq) + 2Br^-(aq) \longrightarrow 2Cl^-(aq) + Br_2(aq)$$
$$Cl_2(aq) + 2I^-(aq) \longrightarrow 2Cl^-(aq) + I_2(aq)$$

■ Bromine displaces iodine:

$$Br_2(aq) + 2I^-(aq) \longrightarrow 2Br^-(aq) + I_2(aq)$$

■ Iodine does not displace either chlorine or bromine.

| Element | $E^{\ominus}_{X_2/2X^-}/V$ |
|---|---|
| chlorine | +1.36 |
| bromine | +1.09 |
| iodine | +0.54 |

● *Table 6.2* Standard electrode potentials of Group VII elements in contact with solutions of their ions

One of the problems with doing these displacement reactions is being able to see if a reaction has taken place – the halide ion solutions are all colourless and very dilute solutions of the halogens can also appear colourless. To avoid this problem, an organic solvent such as hexane or cyclohexane is added to the mixture, which forms a separate layer. The halogens are more soluble in organic solvents than in aqueous solution, so they are taken up by the hexane and the colour is much more apparent. For instance, bromine is a strong orange-yellow colour in hexane, and iodine is purple. So if aqueous bromine is mixed with hexane, the bromine dissolves in the hexane, which turns orange. Then if aqueous potassium iodide is added, the hexane turns purple, which shows us that bromine has become bromide ion and displaced iodine from solution. Try the displacement reactions (indicated in *table 6.3)* in the laboratory, to check the order of reactivity of the halogens.

## SAQ 6.3

From your knowledge of the structure and bonding of the halogens, explain why they are more soluble in organic solvents than in aqueous solution.

The oxidising ability of the halogens means that they are useful in many ways. Chlorine and its aqueous solution, known as chlorine water, are often used as oxidising agents (chlorine water contains chlorine and chloric(I) acid, HClO). Chlorine is also used in industry as a bleach; it oxidises large organic molecules to colourless compounds. In recent years controversy has arisen over the use of chlorine for bleaching paper – although very white paper pulp can be produced, the process results in the formation of dioxins, which are poisonous and can accumulate in living organisms, as dioxins do not break down easily. Nowadays ozone is often used to bleach paper that does not have to be pure white, like tissues, nappies and toilet paper.

The strong oxidising ability of chlorine is also used by the water industry to treat drinking water. Chlorine is added to water from reservoirs to kill any bacteria, and small amounts of chlorine remain in the water piped to consumers to prevent bacterial contamination. Chlorine is also used to keep water in swimming pools free from contamination.

Fluorine is rarely used as an oxidising reagent as it is difficult to handle.

## SAQ 6.4

Bromine water (aqueous bromine, $Br_2$) was shaken with a small volume of cyclohexane, and then the following aqueous solutions were added to separate portions:

a   aqueous sodium iodide,

b   aqueous chlorine,

c   aqueous sodium astatide, NaAt.

Each mixture was shaken again. Describe what you would expect to see. Write equations for any reactions that would occur.

| | Halide | | |
| --- | --- | --- | --- |
| Halogen | Chloride, $Cl^-$ | Bromide, $Br^-$ | Iodide, $I^-$ |
| Chlorine, $Cl_2$ | | orange-yellow bromine released | purple iodine released |
| Bromine, $Br_2$ | no reaction | | purple iodine released |
| Iodine, $I_2$ | no reaction | no reaction | |

● **Table 6.3** Displacement reactions of halogens (the colours refer to the colours of the halogens in cyclohexane)

# The reactions of the halogens with thiosulphate ions

All the halogens react with the thiosulphate ion, $S_2O_3^{2-}$. Chlorine and bromine produce sulphate ions:

$$4Cl_2(aq) + S_2O_3^{2-}(aq) + 5H_2O(l)$$
$$\longrightarrow 2SO_4^{2-}(aq) + 10H^+(aq) + 8Cl^-(aq)$$

Iodine reacts differently because it is less strongly oxidising – tetrathionate ions, $S_4O_6^{2-}$, are produced:

$$I_2(aq) + 2S_2O_3^{2-}(aq) \longrightarrow 2I^-(aq) + S_4O_6^{2-}(aq)$$

This reaction is very important because it is used as a method of estimating the amount of an oxidising agent by titration. To estimate the amount of an oxidising agent:

- Add excess $I^-$ ions to an acidified solution of the oxidising agent; some will be oxidised to $I_2$ according to the amount of oxidising agent present.
- Titrate the $I_2$ with standard aqueous sodium thiosulphate.
- The end-point is detected with starch solution, which forms a dark blue complex with iodine but is colourless in the presence of $I^-$. (Remember to add the starch close to the end-point, otherwise the complex it forms with iodine is insoluble and the end-point is difficult to detect!)

Hydrogen chloride, hydrogen bromide and hydrogen iodide can be prepared in this way:

$$H_2(g) + X_2(g) \longrightarrow 2HX(g)$$
hydrogen    halogen    hydrogen halide

### How does each halogen react with hydrogen?

| | | |
|---|---|---|
| This reaction illustrates decreasing reactivity down the Group | chlorine | Explodes in direct sunlight. Slow reaction in the dark |
| | bromine | Reacts at 300°C and using a platinum catalyst |
| | iodine | Slow reaction at 300°C and using a platinum catalyst. Easily reversible, so a partial product obtained |

● **Table 6.4** Reactions of halogens with hydrogen

**SAQ 6.5**
What is the change in oxidation number of sulphur when thiosulphate ions react with **a** chlorine, **b** iodine?

**SAQ 6.6**
From your knowledge of the properties of the halogens, suggest why chlorine and iodine give different products when reacted with thiosulphate ions.

# The hydrogen halides, HCl, HBr and HI

The production of hydrogen halides is summarised in *table 6.4*. The hydrogen halides are acids. The covalent bond in H–Cl is the strongest, and the bond in H–I the weakest, as shown by the standard bond dissociation enthalpies *(table 6.5)*.

The thermal stability of the hydrogen halides decreases in the same order:

$$HCl > HBr > HI$$

because it is dependent on the bond dissociation enthalpy. However, the acid strength of these compounds has the opposite order:

$$HI > HBr > HCl$$

This is because the strength of the acid depends on the concentration of $H^+$. In HI, the bond is weak, so more easily breaks to give $H^+$, so making a stronger acid.

| Hydrogen halide | Bond dissociation enthalpy; $\Delta H^\ominus_{dissociation\ (HX)}$/kJ mol$^{-1}$ |
|---|---|
| HCl | 432 |
| HBr | 366 |
| HI | 298 |

● **Table 6.5** Bond dissociation enthalpies for hydrogen halides

### Which halide?

Halides are extremely common, so a test to identify which halide is present is very useful. This test is based on the colour of silver halides and the different solubilities of the silver halides in ammonia solution.

- Acidify the unknown halide solution with dilute nitric acid.
- Add silver nitrate solution to precipitate the silver halide:
    silver chloride is white
    silver bromide is cream
    silver iodide is yellow
- Identification by colour is not completely reliable, so add ammonia solution:
    white silver chloride is soluble in dilute ammonia solution;
    cream silver bromide is soluble in concentrated ammonia solution;
    yellow silver iodide is insoluble in concentrated ammonia solution.

# Concentrated sulphuric acid and the halide ions

Concentrated sulphuric acid is an oxidising agent, and halide ions are reducing agents – remember that the halogens $X_2$ are oxidising agents, so the halides $X^-$ are reducing agents. What happens when concentrated sulphuric acid and halide ions react together? A different reaction happens for each halide ion.

When potassium chloride is reacted with concentrated sulphuric acid, hydrogen chloride is produced:

$$KCl(s) + H_2SO_4(l) \longrightarrow HCl(g) + KHSO_4(s)$$

If a similar reaction is used to make hydrogen bromide, the bromide ion produced is oxidised to bromine:

$$2HBr(g) + H_2SO_4(l) \longrightarrow Br_2(l) + SO_2(g) + 2H_2O(l)$$

In this reaction, hydrogen bromide reduces sulphuric acid to sulphur dioxide.

A similar reaction to make hydrogen iodide produces yet another set of products, as the iodide ion reduces concentrated sulphuric acid to hydrogen sulphide:

$$8HI(g) + H_2SO_4(l) \longrightarrow 4I_2(s) + H_2S(g) + 4H_2O(l)$$

You can recognise $H_2S$ by its 'bad egg' smell and by its reaction with lead ethanoate:

$$Pb(CH_3CO_2)_2(aq) + H_2S(g) \longrightarrow 2CH_3CO_2H(aq) + PbS(s)$$

We can see from these reactions that hydrogen iodide is a more powerful reducing agent than hydrogen bromide (if you are not convinced, try the SAQ below and work out the change in oxidation numbers in each reaction). This corresponds to the $E^\ominus$ values of the halogens, which tell us that iodine is the least powerful oxidising agent.

## SAQ 6.7

a  What is the change in oxidation number for (i) chlorine, (ii) bromine, (iii) iodine in the reactions shown above?

b  What is the change in the oxidation number of sulphur in each of the reactions with halide ions?

# The reaction of chlorine with sodium hydroxide

The way in which chlorine reacts with aqueous sodium hydroxide depends on the temperature.

With *cold* (15 °C) dilute aqueous sodium hydroxide a mixture of halide ($Cl^-$) and halate(I) ($ClO^-$) ions is formed:

$$Cl_2(g) + 2NaOH(aq) \longrightarrow NaCl(aq) + NaClO(aq) + H_2O(l)$$

This is an interesting reaction because it demonstrates **disproportionation** – a particular type of redox reaction in which one species is oxidised and reduced at the same time. This happens to the chlorine – the ionic equation shows that the oxidation number of chlorine in the products of the reaction are both lower and higher than chlorine itself:

$$Cl_2 + 2OH^- \longrightarrow Cl^- + ClO^- + H_2O$$

oxidation no. of Cl: 0 → −1 (reduction), +1 (oxidation)

This reaction is used commercially to produce bleach, which is HClO, or hypochlorous acid. You can see this name on some bleach products.

Household bleach is an aqueous solution of sodium chloride and sodium chlorate(I), NaClO, in a one-to-one mole ratio.

With *hot* (70°C) dilute aqueous sodium hydroxide the $ClO^-$ disproportionates further:

$$3ClO^- \longrightarrow 2Cl^- + ClO_3^-$$

oxidation $\quad$ +1 $\qquad$ −1 $\quad$ chlorate(v) ions
no. of Cl $\qquad\qquad\qquad\qquad\qquad$ +5

so that the entire equation is:

$$3Cl_2(g) + 6NaOH(aq)$$
$$\longrightarrow 5NaCl(aq) + NaClO_3(aq) + 3H_2O(l)$$

## SUMMARY

■ The halogens chlorine, bromine and iodine are covalent diatomic molecules at room temperature. They become increasingly less volatile and more deeply coloured on descending Group VII.

■ The halogens have many common characteristics. They are all reactive, and this reactivity decreases on descending the Group.

■ All the halogens are good oxidising agents. Chlorine is the strongest oxidising agent of the three halogens studied – it has the most positive standard electrode potential.

■ The order of reactivity can be determined by displacement reactions. A halogen can displace another with a less positive standard electrode potential.

■ The halogens react with the thiosulphate ion, and this reaction is especially important with iodine, as it is used for the quantitative determination of oxidising agents.

■ The hydrogen halides are acids, and their thermal stability decreases on descending the Group.

■ The identification of a halide ion in solution is made after adding silver nitrate solution and then aqueous ammonia.

■ The reactions of the halide ions with concentrated sulphuric acid show the increasing reducing power of the halide ion on descending the Group.

■ Chlorine reacts with both cold and hot hydroxide ions in a disproportionation reaction. This reaction produces commercial bleach.

■ The halogens all have important industrial uses, especially for chlorine, which is used in the manufacture of many other useful products.

*SAQ 6.8*

What is the ionic equation for the reaction between chlorine and hot dilute sodium hydroxide?

## *Questions*

1 Sodium chlorate(I), found in bleach, decomposes slowly, releasing oxygen.
   a Write the equation for this decomposition.
   b Identify which element has been oxidised and which has been reduced.

2 The standard electrode potential for the $Fe^{3+}/Fe^{2+}$ system is $+0.77\,V$. Which of the halogens will oxidise $Fe^{3+}$ to $Fe^{2+}$ in aqueous solution?

3 Domestic bleach contains sodium chlorate(I), NaClO. In acid solution the chlorate(I) ion reacts with iodide ions to give iodine:

$$ClO^-(aq) + 2H^+(aq) + 2I^-(aq)$$
$$\longrightarrow Cl^-(aq) + I_2(aq) + H_2O(l)$$

The concentration of chlorate(I) ion can be calculated by titrating the iodine against a standard solution of sodium thiosulphate.
   a Write the equation for the reaction between thiosulphate ions and iodine molecules.
   b A $25.0\,cm^3$ sample of domestic bleach was diluted to $250\,cm^3$ with distilled water. A $25.0\,cm^3$ portion of the diluted bleach was then acidified and treated with potassium iodide solution to ensure that all the chlorate(I) ions reacted. The iodine liberated was titrated against standard sodium thiosulphate solution, $0.20\,mol\,dm^{-3}$; it was found that $19.8\,cm^3$ of the thiosulphate solution was required. Calculate the concentration of chlorate(I) in domestic bleach.

# Chapter seven

# The transition elements and their compounds

### By the end of this chapter you should be able to:

1 recall the definition of a transition element;

2 explain the variable oxidation states of transition elements in terms of the filling and energy levels of the 3d and 4s electron subshells;

3 explain why the transition elements and their compounds can be successful catalysts;

4 explain why scandium and zinc are not transition elements, despite their location in the d block of the Periodic Table;

5 describe how transition elements form complexes, and define the terms *ligand* and *coordination number*;

6 describe the process of ligand displacement, with particular reference to the complexes of the copper(II) ion;

7 explain how colour is produced in transition element complexes.

## Introduction

The transition elements are found in the d block of the Periodic Table, located between Groups II and III. However, not all d-block elements are transition elements. There is a particular definition of a transition element:

A transition element is an element that forms at least one ion with a partially filled d subshell.

The transition elements have certain common physical properties:

■ they are metals with high melting points;

■ they are hard and rigid, and so are useful as constructional materials;

■ they are good conductors of electricity.

They also have certain common chemical properties:

■ they can show several different oxidation states in their compounds;

■ they are good catalysts;

■ they form coloured compounds;

■ they form complexes with ligands (for an explanation of *ligand*, see page 64).

The physical properties of the transition elements can all be explained by the strong metallic bonding that exists in these elements. There are more electrons in the outer shell of atoms of transition elements than in the outer shell of Group I and Group II metals, so the delocalised sea of electrons typical of metallic bonding produces a strong force holding the positive ions together. The melting points of the transition elements are high because it takes a lot of energy to disrupt this strong metallic bonding. This bonding also explains the good electrical conductivity, as there are many mobile electrons present. The hardness of the transition elements is caused by the atoms being held firmly in place by the metallic bonding.

It is worth noting here, before we continue, that many of the elements in the f block are also transition elements. In this book we will consider only the first row of d-block elements, from scandium to zinc.

## Electronic structures

The electronic structures of the d-block elements dictate their chemistry, and so are extremely important.

| | | |
|---|---|---|
| scandium | Sc | $[Ar]3d^14s^2$ |
| titanium | Ti | $[Ar]3d^24s^2$ |
| vanadium | V | $[Ar]3d^34s^2$ |
| chromium | Cr | $[Ar]3d^54s^1$ |
| manganese | Mn | $[Ar]3d^54s^2$ |
| iron | Fe | $[Ar]3d^64s^2$ |
| cobalt | Co | $[Ar]3d^74s^2$ |
| nickel | Ni | $[Ar]3d^84s^2$ |
| copper | Cu | $[Ar]3d^{10}4s^1$ |
| zinc | Zn | $[Ar]3d^{10}4s^2$ |

If you look at these electronic configurations, you will see that the d subshell is being filled as we move from scandium to zinc, hence the term 'd block' – scandium has one d electron, and zinc has ten, a full d subshell. The 3d level is filled before the 4s level because it becomes lower in energy than the 4s level at scandium, and the 3d electrons feel a slightly stronger attraction for the nucleus than the 4s electrons. But the two levels remain *very close in energy*. We see this closeness illustrated in chromium and copper. Chromium, instead of having a $[Ar]3d^44s^2$ structure, has $[Ar]3d^54s^1$; it has two *half-filled* subshells, which gives it greater stability. This exchange is made possible by the closeness of the two subshells. Similarly, copper has a full d subshell and a half-filled 4s shell: $[Ar]3d^{10}4s^1$.

# Variable oxidation states

Transition elements occur in multiple oxidation states. The most common oxidation state is +2, which occurs when the two 4s electrons are lost (for example $Fe^{2+}$ and $Co^{2+}$). But because the 3d electrons are very close in energy to the 4s electrons they can quite easily be lost too, so one element can form several different ions by losing different numbers of electrons, and all the ions will be almost equally stable. This similarity in energy between the 3d and 4s electrons also explains why the transition elements have such similar properties to each other.

*Table 7.1* shows the main oxidation states of the first row of the d-block elements. The commonly occurring oxidation states are underlined. It is worth noting that a common oxidation state for the first five elements is the same as the total number of 4s and 3d electrons for the element; and for the second five elements, a common oxidation state is +2.

Take a look at the electronic configurations of the first element, scandium, and the last element, zinc. For scandium the only

possible oxidation state is +3, so the ion is $Sc^{3+}$, with the electronic configuration [Ar]. This ion has no d electrons, so does not satisfy the definition of a transition element – scandium is a d-block element but is *not* a transition element. Now look at zinc. The only possible ion is $Zn^{2+}$, with the electronic configuration $[Ar]3d^{10}$. This ion does not have a partially filled d subshell – so zinc is *not* a transition element. This is the reason why the compounds of zinc and scandium are white, and not coloured like those of transition elements (see page 67).

In transition element chemistry, the changes in oxidation state of the ions are often shown by changes in the colour of the solutions. For example, potassium dichromate(VI) is often used in titrations:

$$\underset{\text{orange}}{Cr_2O_7{}^{2-}(aq)} + 14H^+(aq) + 6e^-$$
$$\longrightarrow \underset{\text{blue–violet}}{2Cr^{3+}(aq)} + 7H_2O(l)$$

## SAQ 7.1

What is the oxidation number of chromium in **a** $Cr_2O_7{}^{2-}$ and **b** $Cr^{3+}$?

# Transition elements as catalysts

A catalyst is a substance that speeds up a chemical reaction, without itself being permanently changed in a chemical way. Many transition elements are effective catalysts, and are used in reactions both in the laboratory and in industry.

| Element | Oxidation states | | | | | |
|---|---|---|---|---|---|---|
| Sc | | | +<u>3</u> | | | |
| Ti | | +2 | +<u>3</u> | +<u>4</u> | | |
| V | | +2 | +<u>3</u> | +4 | +<u>5</u> | |
| Cr | | +2 | +<u>3</u> | +4 | +5 | +<u>6</u> |
| Mn | | +<u>2</u> | +3 | +<u>4</u> | +5 | +6 | +<u>7</u> |
| Fe | | +<u>2</u> | +<u>3</u> | +4 | +5 | +6 |
| Co | | +<u>2</u> | +<u>3</u> | +4 | +5 |
| Ni | | +<u>2</u> | +3 | +4 |
| Cu | +<u>1</u> | +2 | +3 |
| Zn | | +2 |

● *Table 7.1* Oxidation states of the first row of d-block elements; the most common oxidation states are shown underlined

## Box 7A Catalysis

Catalysts can be divided into two groups, homogeneous and heterogeneous. A **homogeneous** catalyst is in the same phase as the reactants (such as a gas catalyst for a gas reaction), whereas a **heterogeneous** catalyst is in a different phase from the reactants (such as a solid catalyst for a liquid reaction).

Industrial catalysts are often heterogeneous *(table 7.2)*. The first way in which they operate is adsorption, or attachment, of the reactant on to the surface of the catalyst. In **physisorption** the reactant molecule is attached to the catalyst surface by weak van der Waals forces. In **chemisorption** the reactant forms a chemical bond with the surface, and dissociation of the reactant often occurs *(figure 7.1)*. This leaves the reactant molecule more readily available to react.

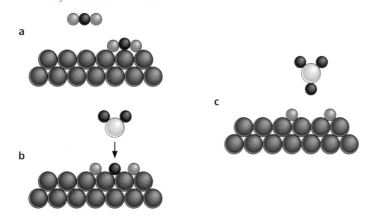

● *Figure 7.1* Chemisorption on the surface of a catalyst.
**a** A reactant molecule bonds to the surface.
**b** The molecule dissociates and another reactant molecule approaches.
**c** The second molecule removes one of the dissociated atoms.

Without catalysts, it would be much more difficult to make many products that we use routinely. The Nobel prize winners Karl Ziegler and Giulio Natta discovered a metal-catalysed polymerisation reaction that enables us to make poly(alkenes), particularly poly(ethene), easily and at relatively low pressures. The catalyst is a complex made from titanium tetrachloride and triethylaluminium.

In the laboratory, you may have seen the decomposition of hydrogen peroxide to water and oxygen:

$$2H_2O_2(l) \longrightarrow 2H_2O(l) + O_2(g)$$

At room temperature this reaction is very slow. However, if manganese(IV) oxide is added it acts as a catalyst, and the reaction becomes very rapid.

In industry, one of the best-known reactions that depends on a catalyst is the Haber process, in which nitrogen and hydrogen react to give ammonia:

$$N_2(g) + 3H_2(g) \rightleftharpoons 2NH_3(g)$$

The catalyst used in this reaction is finely divided iron, or iron(III) oxide, $Fe_2O_3$.

Transition elements make efficient catalysts for two reasons:
■ they can have several different oxidation states, so they can participate in electron transfer reactions, thus providing an alternative route for a reaction in a way that lowers the activation energy and so speeds up the reaction;

| Reaction | Type of catalysis | Catalyst |
|---|---|---|
| Haber process (production of ammonia) $N_2(g) + 3H_2(g) \rightleftharpoons 2NH_3(g)$ | heterogeneous | finely divided iron or iron(III) oxide |
| Contact process (production of sulphuric acid) $2SO_2(g) + O_2(g) \rightleftharpoons 2SO_3(g)$ | heterogeneous | solid vanadium(V) oxide |
| hydrogenation of alkenes | heterogeneous | finely divided nickel |
| laboratory preparation of oxygen $2H_2O_2(l) \longrightarrow 2H_2O(l) + O_2(g)$ | heterogeneous | solid manganese(IV) oxide |

● *Table 7.2* Some examples of the use of transition elements and their compounds as catalysts

■ they provide sites at which reactions can take place – transition elements can bond to a wide range of ions and molecules, and can have different numbers of bonds, so the reacting molecules can be held in place while the reaction occurs.

# Complexes

Transition elements form **complexes**, or **coordination compounds**, with ligands. **Ligands** are electron-pair donors and they form dative or coordinate covalent bonds with the central transition element ion.

Ligands are either anions or neutral molecules. If the ligand donates one pair of electrons to the ion it is called a **monodentate** ligand. **Polydentate** ligands have more than one site that bonds to the metal ion – for example, bidentate ligands donate two pairs of electrons (they bond in two places)

and hexadentate ligands donate six pairs of electrons. *Table 7.3* lists some examples of ligands.

The formula of a complex is always written with the central transition element ion first, followed by the ligands, and with the overall charge of the ion at the end, for example $[Ni(CN)_4]^{2-}$ and $[Cr(H_2O)_4Cl_2]^+$. The overall charge on the complex is simply the individual charges of the transition element ion and the ligands added together. In these two examples, we know that the ligands must be $CN^-$, $Cl^-$ and $H_2O$, so we can work out that the transition element ions are $Ni^{2+}$ and $Cr^{3+}$.

## SAQ 7.2

What are the formulas and charges of the complexes made from the following ions?

a   One nickel(II) ion and four bromide ions.

b   One iron(II) ion and six chloride ions.

| Type of ligand | Formula | Name |
|---|---|---|
| monodentate | $H_2O$ | water |
|  | $NH_3$ | ammonia |
|  | CO | carbon monoxide |
|  | $Cl^-$ | chloride ion |
|  | $Br^-$ | bromide ion |
|  | $CN^-$ | cyanide ion |
|  | $OH^-$ | hydroxide ion |
|  | $S^{2-}$ | sulphide ion |
|  | $NO_2^-$ | nitrite ion |
|  | $SCN^-$ | thiocyanate ion |
|  | $S_2O_3^{2-}$ | thiosulphate ion |
| bidentate | $NH_2CH_2CH_2NH_2$ | ethane-1,2-diamine |
|  | $CO_2^-$ $\vert$ $CO_2^-$ | ethanedioate ion |
| hexadentate | | edta (ethylenediaminetetraacetic acid) ion |

● *Table 7.3*  Some of the more common ligands

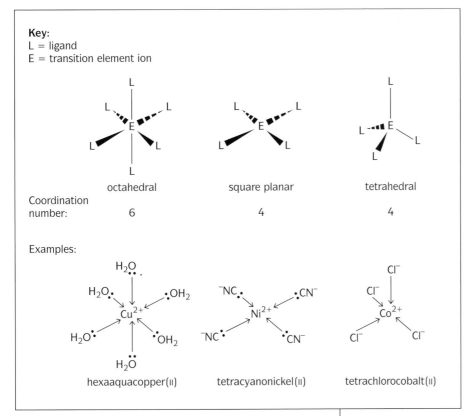

Key:
L = ligand
E = transition element ion

| octahedral | square planar | tetrahedral |
| --- | --- | --- |
| Coordination number: 6 | 4 | 4 |

Examples:

hexaaquacopper(II)    tetracyanonickel(II)    tetrachlorocobalt(II)

● **Figure 7.2** The shapes of transition element complexes.

## Shapes of complexes

The number of lone-pairs of electrons bonded to the transition element ion is called the **coordination number** of the complex. This is related to the shape of the complex. There are three main shapes adopted by transition element complexes – octahedral, tetrahedral and square planar *(figure 7.2)*. An octahedral complex has a coordination number of 6, and the other two shapes both have a coordination number of 4.

One of the best-known complexes is formed in a solution of copper(II) sulphate, $CuSO_4$. In aqueous solution the copper ion is not isolated, but forms a complex with six water molecules. The complex has an octahedral shape, as shown in *figure 7.2*. This complex is responsible for the blue colour associated with copper sulphate solution.

## Ligand displacement

The water ligands in the copper complex of aqueous copper(II) sulphate can be displaced by other ligands to form a more stable complex.

● **Figure 7.3** The structure of the tetraamminecopper(II) complex.

When concentrated hydrochloric acid is added drop by drop, the solution turns yellow as a new complex is formed – four water ligands are replaced by four chloride ion ligands to give $[CuCl_4]^{2-}$:

$$[Cu(H_2O)_6]^{2+}(aq) + 4HCl(aq)$$
$$\longrightarrow [CuCl_4]^{2-}(aq) + 6H_2O(l) + 4H^+(aq)$$

The chloride ion ligands are similarly replaced by ammonia ligands when concentrated ammonia solution is added drop by drop (producing a deep-blue solution):

$$[CuCl_4]^{2-}(aq) + 4NH_3(aq) + 2H_2O(l)$$
$$\longrightarrow [Cu(NH_3)_4(H_2O)_2]^{2+}(aq) + 4Cl^-(aq)$$

*Figure 7.3* shows the structure of the octahedral complex. The ammonia ions can also be replaced, by edta *(box 7B)*, to give a complex that is turquoise in aqueous solution.

This sequence of ligand replacement means that we can list the complexes in order according to their stability *(table 7.4)*.

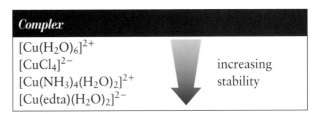

| Complex | |
| --- | --- |
| $[Cu(H_2O)_6]^{2+}$ | |
| $[CuCl_4]^{2-}$ | increasing |
| $[Cu(NH_3)_4(H_2O)_2]^{2+}$ | stability |
| $[Cu(edta)(H_2O)_2]^{2-}$ | |

● **Table 7.4** The stability of copper complexes

## Box 7B  Edta

The anion edta$^{4-}$ is hexadentate – it has six available electron-pairs. Edta acts as a kind of cage and 'traps' a metal ion inside it to form a very stable complex *(figure 7.4)*; sometimes complexes like this are called **chelates**, from the Greek for crab's claw. Edta can be used in many situations to 'mop up' metal ions. For example:

- it is used in trace amounts in some foods to prevent metal ions catalysing the reaction that makes fats rancid;
- it is added to shampoos to help soften the water;
- it is used as a cleaning agent in disinfectants;
- it is used in medicine to prevent blood from clotting during operations, by chelating with calcium ions.

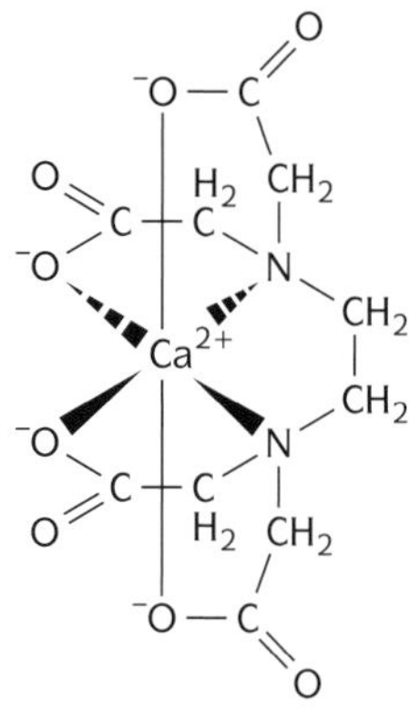

● **Figure 7.4** Edta chelation of a calcium ion.

## Gelatinous precipitates

When excess ammonia is added slowly to aqueous copper(II) sulphate, a pale blue precipitate is first seen:

$$[Cu(H_2O)_6]^{2+}(aq) + 2NH_3(aq)$$
$$\longrightarrow [Cu(H_2O)_4(OH)_2](s) + 2NH_4^+(aq)$$

This pale blue precipitate is copper(II) hydroxide. Many transition elements form insoluble metal hydroxides, and because these precipitates often resemble a jelly they are called gelatinous precipitates. They can be formed by adding aqueous sodium hydroxide to the aqueous transition element ion. For example:

$$Mn^{2+}(aq) + 2OH^-(aq) \longrightarrow Mn(OH)_2(s)$$
$$\text{cream}$$

$$Cr^{3+}(aq) + 3OH^-(aq) \longrightarrow Cr(OH)_3(s)$$
$$\text{grey–green}$$

But as we have seen, gelatinous precipitates can also be formed when ammonia solution is added to the aqueous transition element ion. This is because ammonia is a weak base that exists in equilibrium with the hydroxide ion in aqueous solution:

$$NH_3(aq) + H_2O(l) \rightleftharpoons NH_4^+(aq) + OH^-(aq)$$

so aqueous ammonia is a source of both hydroxide ions and ammonia ligands. For example, aqueous ammonia added to $Mn^{2+}(aq)$ gives a yellowish precipitate of $Mn(OH)_2$, and not a complex with ammonia ligands as you might expect. However, in the case of copper hydroxide, further addition of aqueous ammonia does produce the complex, as the precipitate dissolves in aqueous ammonia to give a deep-blue solution:

$$[Cu(H_2O)_4(OH)_2](aq) + 4NH_3(aq)$$
$$\longrightarrow [Cu(H_2O)_2(NH_3)_4]^{2+}(aq) + 2H_2O(l) + 2OH^-(aq)$$

This complex is also octahedral in shape.

### SAQ 7.3

Predict what will happen when aqueous ammonia is added to aqueous solutions of **a** $Fe^{2+}$, **b** $Fe^{3+}$ and **c** $Cr^{3+}$.

### SAQ 7.4

Draw the $[Ni(H_2O)_6]^{2+}$ complex, showing the shape clearly. What is the coordination number of the $Ni^{2+}$ ion in this complex?

## Coloured compounds

Transition element complexes in aqueous solution are frequently coloured:

| | |
|---|---|
| $Fe^{2+}$ | green |
| $Fe^{3+}$ | yellow |
| $Cu^{2+}$ | blue |
| $Ni^{2+}$ | green |
| $Co^{2+}$ | pink |
| $Ti^{3+}$ | purple |
| $Cr^{3+}$ | violet |
| $Mn^{2+}$ | pink |

This colour is related to the presence of unpaired electrons in the d orbitals; for this reason, an ion with a full d subshell will not be coloured. This is shown by the complexes of zinc, in which the ion $Zn^{2+}$ has a full $d^{10}$ subshell.

## *The production of colour*

1 The d orbitals are split into two sets with different energies (higher and lower) when a ligand forms a complex with a transition element ion. The transition element ion in solution is never found in isolation, as water can always be a ligand, so the d orbitals are always split.

2 When light energy falls on the complex, it can be absorbed by the d electrons.

3 Using this energy, the d electrons can be promoted to the higher energy levels.

4 When the electrons return to their original, lower level, they transmit the light they originally absorbed. This light falls in the visible region, so we see a coloured compound.

The colour of a complex is affected by
■ the number of d electrons present, and
■ which ligands are present.

---

### Box 7C  Stereoisomerism

If a transition element complex has two different kinds of ligand, it is possible that the ligands can be arranged in different ways to produce detectably different spatial structures. This is stereoisomerism.

One type of stereoisomerism seen in transition element complexes is *cis–trans* isomerism *(figure 7.5)*. You can see the difference between the isomers very clearly if you make molecular models. You will find that the isomers cannot be superimposed on each other.

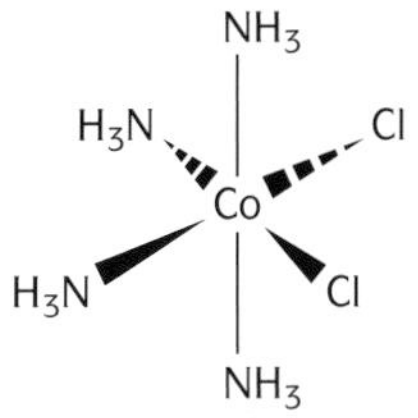

*cis*-isomer

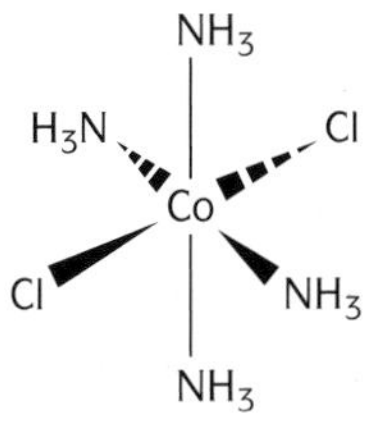

*trans*-isomer

● *Figure 7.5 Cis–trans* isomerism in the tetraamminedichlorocobalt(II) complex.

## SUMMARY

■ The transition elements all have at least one ion with a partially filled d subshell of electrons.

■ Transition elements all have several oxidation states because the s electrons and d electrons are close in energy. This makes them successful catalysts.

■ Scandium and zinc are d-block elements, but are not transition elements. This is because they do not form ions with a partially filled d subshell. The compounds of scandium and zinc are colourless.

■ Transition elements form complexes with ligands. Ligands form a dative covalent bond to the transition element ion.

■ Many complexes have six ligands and are octahedrally shaped; complexes with four ligands can be tetrahedral or square planar in shape.

■ The number of lone-pairs of electrons bonded to the transition element ion is called the coordination number of the complex.

■ The ligands in transition element complexes can displace each other.

■ Transition element complexes are usually coloured. The colours depend on the electron energy levels in the partially filled d subshell, and are affected by the number of electrons present and the type(s) of ligands in the complex.

## Questions

1  a  Write down the electron configurations of $V^{3+}$, $Ni^{2+}$ and $Cu^+$.
   b  Look up values for the first ionisation energies of the first row of the transition elements. Comment on these values.

2  a  Chromium is chemically unreactive. Suggest a reason for this.
   b  Copper(I) compounds are not strongly coloured. Explain why.

3  a  The complex $[Ni(H_2O)_2(NH_3)_4]^{2+}$ is green in aqueous solution. Draw the structure(s) of this complex, and write down its coordination number.
   b  Calculate the oxidation number of the transition element in:
      (i) $Cr(CO)_6$
      (ii) $[TiF_6]^{2-}$
      (iii) $[Cu(CN)_4]^{3-}$
      (iv) $[Co(NO_3)_4]^{2-}$

# Answers to self-assessment questions

## Chapter 1

1.1 Hydrogen bonding and electrostatic attraction.

1.2 **a** He atoms **b** $O_2$ molecules

    **c** $N_2$ molecules

1.3 **a** Average speed increases.

    **b** Pressure increases.

    **c** Pressure decreases.

1.4 Hydrogen bonding in ethanoic acid vapour means that the ideal gas assumption of no forces between molecules does not apply. There is no such bonding in helium, so its behaviour is close to ideal.

1.5 $0.6\,m^3$

1.6 $0.17\,dm^3$

1.7 $522\,K$

1.8 $70\,g\,mol^{-1}$

1.9 Sand consists mainly of quartz, which is a silicate. It has a giant structure held together by covalent bonds, so it is difficult to break apart.

1.10 $2Al(s) + \frac{3}{2}O_2(g) \longrightarrow Al_2O_3(s)$

1.11 Mining the ore, concentrating the mineral and reducing the mineral all use energy. Recycled metal does not require these steps, hence the energy is saved. If the metal is wasted, the proportion of energy needed to maintain the cycle is increased. This is economically and environmentally undesirable.

## Chapter 2

2.1 **a** Reduction **b** Reduction **c** Oxidation

    **d** Neither **e** Oxidation **f** Both

2.2 **a** Mg oxidised, $Zn^{2+}$ reduced.

    **b** Zn oxidised, $Pb^{2+}$ reduced.

    **c** C oxidised, $Cu^{2+}$ reduced.

2.3 $Mg(s) + 2H_2O(g) \longrightarrow Mg(OH)_2(aq) + H_2(g)$

2.4 **a** $Mg(s) + H_2SO_4(aq)$
$\longrightarrow MgSO_4(aq) + H_2(g)$
Mg oxidised, $H^+$ reduced.

    **b** $2Na(s) + H_2SO_4(aq)$
$\longrightarrow Na_2SO_4(aq) + H_2(g)$
Na oxidised, $H^+$ reduced.

    **c** $2Na(s) + 2HCl(aq) \longrightarrow 2NaCl(aq) + H_2(g)$
Na oxidised, $H^+$ reduced.

2.5 $Al(s) + 3HCl(aq) \longrightarrow AlCl_3(aq) + \frac{3}{2}H_2(g)$

    $Fe(s) + 2HCl(aq) \longrightarrow FeCl_2(aq) + H_2(g)$

    Silver does not react.

2.6 $Zn(s) + Pb^{2+}(aq) \longrightarrow Zn^{2+}(aq) + Pb(s)$

2.7 Copper wire dissolves, silver is precipitated.

2.8 The mass decreases as the zinc electrode dissolves.

2.9 Filter paper is cheaper and more readily available, but must not be allowed to dry out and must be freshly prepared for each cell. The glass tube filled with agar is more difficult to prepare, but is easier to use and only needs replenishing periodically.

2.10 Nitrate ions move to the zinc half-cell.

2.11 **a** Magnesium **b** See *figure*.

    **c** 1.61 V **d** Zinc

    **e** Magnesium $\longrightarrow$ zinc

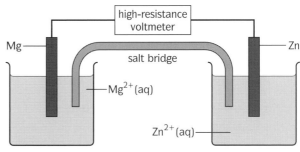

● *Answer for* SAQ 2.11b

**2.12** $Zn(s)|Zn^{2+}(aq) \parallel Ag^+(aq)|Ag(s)$

$E^{\ominus} = 1.56\,V$

**2.13 a** $Co(s) \longrightarrow Co^{2+}(aq) + 2e^-$

$Ni^{2+}(aq) + 2e^- \longrightarrow Ni(s)$

Full equation:

$Co(s) + Ni^{2+}(aq) \longrightarrow Co^{2+}(aq) + Ni(s)$

**b** $Fe^{2+}(aq) \longrightarrow Fe^{3+}(aq) + e^-$

$Ag^+(aq) + e^- \longrightarrow Ag(s)$

Full equation:

$Fe^{2+}(aq) + Ag^+(aq) \longrightarrow Fe^{3+}(aq) + Ag(s)$

**c** $Cr(s) \longrightarrow Cr^{3+}(aq) + 3e^-$

$Fe^{2+}(aq) + 2e^- \longrightarrow Fe(s)$

Full equation:

$2Cr(s) + 3Fe^{2+}(aq) \longrightarrow 2Cr^{3+}(aq) + 3Fe(s)$

**2.14** Positive

**2.15** Positive terminal: $Fe^{2+}(aq) + 2e^- \longrightarrow Fe(s)$

Negative terminal: $Mg(s) \longrightarrow Mg^{2+}(aq) + 2e^-$

# Chapter 3

**3.1** Cathode: $K^+(l) + e^- \longrightarrow K(s)$

Anode: $2Br^-(l) \longrightarrow Br_2(l) + 2e^-$

**3.2** $Cu^{2+}$

**3.3 a** The blue colour is due to the presence of $Cu^{2+}$ ions; these are discharged during electrolysis to form copper.

**b** The bubbles are of hydrogen gas, because when all the copper ions have been discharged, water molecules are discharged.

**c** When the anode has disappeared.

**3.4** $1+$

**3.5** $5.40\,g$ lead, $314\,cm^3$ oxygen.

**3.6 a** The gain in mass at the cathode will be the same as the loss in mass at the anode.

**b** So that an average difference in mass can be taken if necessary.

**c** Current will not flow if the copper is coated with oxide.

**d** $mol^{-1}$

# Chapter 4

**4.1** Electronegativity increases going down the Group, due to the addition of outer shells of electrons.

**4.2** There is a large increase from the second to the third ionisation energies, indicating that two outer-shell electrons have been removed and the next (third) electron comes from an inner shell.

**4.3** $Mg(s) + 2H^+(aq) \longrightarrow Mg^{2+}(aq) + H_2(g)$

The oxidation number of magnesium increases by 2, that of hydrogen decreases by 1.

**4.4** Magnesium oxide.
$0.33\,g$

**4.5** The stability of the hydroxides increases as the Group is descended, because the cation has a lower charge density and polarises the anion to a lesser extent.

**4.6** The solubility decreases as the Group is descended.

# Chapter 5

**5.1** Yes: tin and lead have a typically metallic, shiny appearance, but carbon (either graphite or diamond) does not look metallic.

**5.2** No – tin displaces lead.

**5.3** See *figure*.

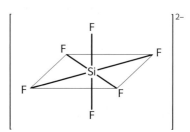

● *Answer for* SAQ 5.3

5.4 Electron-pair repulsion theory predicts that four covalent bonds and no lone-pairs will give a tetrahedral shape.

5.5 The element–hydrogen bond length increases and the bond strength decreases.

5.6 Nitric acid – lead(II) nitrate is soluble. If sulphuric acid is used, insoluble lead(II) sulphate is formed; likewise insoluble lead(II) chloride is formed if hydrochloric acid is used.

5.7 Yes, this is a redox reaction. Sulphur is oxidised and lead is reduced.

# Chapter 6

6.1 $0, -1, +7, +4$

6.2 See *figure*.

$$\left[ \text{Na} \right]^+ \left[ \begin{array}{c} \times\times \\ \times \, \text{Cl} \, \times \\ \bullet\, \, \bullet \\ \times\times \end{array} \right]^-$$

$$\text{H} \, {}^\times_\bullet \, \text{Cl} \, {}^{\bullet\bullet}_{\bullet\bullet}$$

● **Answer for** SAQ 6.2

6.3 The halogens have covalent bonding and they are non-polar molecules. Polar molecules dissolve best in water, which is itself polar. Non-polar molecules dissolve best in non-polar solvents.

6.4 **a** The orange cyclohexane layer would turn purple:
$$Br_2(aq) + 2I^-(aq) \longrightarrow 2Br^-(aq) + I_2(aq)$$

**b** No change.

**c** Given its position in Group VII, we would expect astatine to be darker in colour than iodine. The orange cyclohexane would turn this dark colour of astatine:
$$Br_2(aq) + 2As^-(aq)$$
$$\longrightarrow 2Br^-(aq) + As_2(aq)$$

6.5 **a** $+4\ (+2 \longrightarrow +6)$

**b** $+0.5\ (+2 \longrightarrow +2.5)$

6.6 Chlorine is a stronger oxidising agent than iodine, so it can produce a greater increase in oxidation number than iodine.

6.7 **a** (i) $0\ (-1 \longrightarrow -1)$

(ii) $+1\ (-1 \longrightarrow 0)$

(iii) $+1\ (-1 \longrightarrow 0)$

**b** 0 with chlorine $(+6 \longrightarrow +6)$

$-2$ with bromine $(+6 \longrightarrow +4)$

$-8$ with iodine $(+6 \longrightarrow -2)$

6.8 $3Cl_2(aq) + 6OH^-(aq)$
$$\longrightarrow 5Cl^-(aq) + ClO_3{}^-(aq) + 3H_2O(l)$$

# Chapter 7

7.1 **a** $+6$

**b** $+3$

7.2 **a** $[Ni(Br)_4]^{2-}$

**b** $[Fe(Cl)_6]^{4-}$

7.3 **a** A precipitate of iron(II) hydroxide, $Fe(OH)_2$, is formed.

**b** A precipitate of iron(III) hydroxide, $Fe(OH)_3$, is formed.

**c** A precipitate of chromium(III) hydroxide, $Cr(OH)_3$, is formed.

7.4 *See figure.*

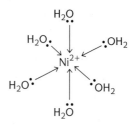

● **Answer for** SAQ 7.4

The coordination number is 6.

---

# Index (Numbers in italics refer to figures.)